Successful Television Management: the Hybrid Approach

Suzana Žilič Fišer

Successful Television Management: the Hybrid Approach

PL ACADEMIC RESEARCH

Bibliographic Information published by the Deutsche Nationalbibliothek
The Deutsche Nationalbibliothek lists this publication in the Deutsche Nationalbibliografie; detailed bibliographic data is available in the internet at http://dnb.d-nb.de.

Library of Congress Cataloging-in-Publication Data
Fišer, Suzana Žilič, 1970-
Successful television management : the hybrid approach / Suzana Žilič Fišer.
pages cm
Includes bibliographical references and index.
ISBN 978-3-631-66306-6
1. Television broadcasting–Europe–Management. 2. Television broadcasting–Europe–Case studies. I. Title.
HE8700.9.E8.F58 2015
384.55068–dc23
2015006666

translator: Zvezdana Marija Kompara
language consultant: Marcus Ferrar

ISBN 978-3-631-66306-6 (Print)
E-ISBN 978-3-653-05542-9 (E-Book)
DOI 10.3726/978-3-653-05542-9

PL Academic Research is an Imprint of Peter Lang GmbH.

Peter Lang – Frankfurt am Main · Bern · Bruxelles · New York · Oxford · Warszawa · Wien

This publication has been peer reviewed.

www.peterlang.com

Table of Contents

Foreword ... 9

1. Introduction ... 11
   Objectives of the Study ... 13
   Why a case study of a hybrid model of broadcasting ... 16

2. Media Organization in Society ... 21
   Mass Media ... 23
   Functions of the media ... 25
   Public interest in all media ... 27
   Media institutions ... 29
   Performance of media policy ... 31
   Broadcasting and aspects of the study ... 32
   Complementary role of public-service broadcasters ... 35

3. Management of Media Organization ... 39
   Modern theories on the organization's management ... 39
   Success of media organization ... 42
   Management of public sector ... 43
   Public versus private sector ... 46
   Media organization ... 48
   Dilemmas of broadcasting policy ... 49
   Management of a public service broadcaster ... 50

4. Broadcasting Systems ... 59
   Commercial dependency and light-touch state regulation in the US ... 60
   Commercial TV stations ... 61
   Public broadcasting service in the US ... 63
   European dual broadcasting system ... 66
   Commercial broadcasters ... 70
   Public-service broadcasters ... 72
   Trends in the dual broadcasting system ... 76
   TV system in the UK ... 79
   BBC as an incumbent public service broadcaster ... 80
   Commercial television ... 81

Hybrid broadcasting model 82
Unique identity of Channel 4 in the British media market 87
Independent production companies 87

5. Evaluating the Performance of Media Organizations 89
Public support for public television 90
Assessment of the broadcasting service operation 92
Traditional criteria for a broadcaster's success 93
The role and significance of economic criteria for performance effectiveness 95
Criteria for studying performance effectivity of commercial broadcasters 96
Criteria for studying performance effectivity of public service broadcasters 97
Common economic criteria for studying performance effectivity of public and commercial media 98

6. Analysis of the Management of a Hybrid TV Model 103
Political criteria versus economic criteria 103
Political criteria 104
Programme strategy of Channel 4 based on political criteria 106
Economic criteria 107
Market-share criteria 107
Management strategies according to market-share criteria 109
Criteria of productivity 109
Management strategies according to criteria of productivity 110
Financial criteria 111
Management strategies according to financial criteria 113
Management criteria 113
Management strategies according to management criteria 116
The positioning of Channel 4 in the British media market 118
Channel 4's environmental context 121

7. Applicability of Management Methods of a Hybrid Broadcasting Model 127
Useful approaches in media management 131
Applicability of a hybrid-broadcasting model to RTV Slovenia 133
Public broadcasting service RTV Slovenia 134
Modern management approaches for RTV Slovenija 136
Context of the public service RTV Slovenija 139

8. Conclusion 141

Summary 143

Enclosures 147

Literature 151

Tables and Figures 163

Foreword

Media have been following and co-shaping social changes since their beginning. With social development, many typical platforms of the last century are becoming obsolete and irrelevant. New media in different forms bring different experiences to the users, which affect production in both traditional and modern media organizations. Advanced consumption of media products imposes new obligations on media organizations and requires additional parameters for the analysis of media institutions facing dynamic media market competition. This book is a sequel to the book Broadcasting Management (Suzana Žilič Fišer, 2007) in which different suppositions and experience of previous studies aim to apply to various media. The book explores a hybrid model of broadcasting in terms of the setting of research parameters and implementation of modern managerial practices, which are suggested as relevant also for the public TV broadcasting stations operating in a market-driven environment. RTV Slovenija is a public TV broadcasting service that exercises the mission of public good. At the same time, it also operates in the media market earning a large share of revenues by advertising. Coordination between the public and economic interests is the key managerial practice used by the public TV broadcasting service.

Changes in society are also transforming the role of social institutions. Media and media institutions most certainly play an important role in democratic society. Due to their dynamic nature, they are forced to coordinate various demands by the public, owners, advertisers and the society. That is why their management has become an extremely complex process. Achieving successful operation requires taking account of different interests, technological development, changes in the regulatory framework and social trends. Media performance reflects social developments, while their management often represents catching of the uncatchable: providing for the public good and offering attractive market products. This book asks several questions and faces many dilemmas. However, it also shows ways how to realize such a complex managerial process and objectives, for the good of all stakeholders. Proof that media can play a positive role also in the market-driven environment can be found in some relevant findings from the field of media, public TV broadcasters, media structure, management and examples of good management practices in electronic media organizations that are presented in this study. However, when looking for successful solutions, it is crucial to be aware of all the traps set by offering either long-term programme contents or merely explicit commercial contents.

In collecting material and writing this book, the author focused on the essence of media performance revealed not only by academic research but also by practical experience in media production. Equipped with experience in Slovenian media production, the author also attentively followed surveys on the British media environment. Colleagues at the BBC and, in particular on Channel 4, as well as many other media professionals were extremely helpful in achieving the goal. The author is very grateful to the British Council and the British Embassy in Slovenia, which financially supported her research work in Great Britain. Working in the media industry enabled the author to conduct more applied research work supported by distinguished professors from Slovenia and other countries. The book also reflects a tendency for networking between the research community and professional performance in the media production.

An important guideline in writing this book was the author's view on media organizations as institutions for societal development and progress. However, the latter can be possible only when a medium observes social values, plays a supervisory role over societal actors and responsibly exerts its power of influence. Any media organization can successfully operate in the market if it transparently exercises the objectives of public and economic interests. Modern managerial approaches can serve this end, since they could be efficient tools to foster a quality media environment that contributes to the development of the whole society.

1. Introduction

The media environment has experienced considerable changes driven by technological, economic and political forces over the last decade. The characteristics of performance are changing and consequently organizations have to adapt continually. A television broadcasting industry governed by a market-oriented rationale is heavily dependent on both the rapidly changing environment and media players within and outside national borders. Overlap between media industries, mergers and acquisitions, removal of legal barriers, the growth of strategic alliances and partnerships among media companies, as well as the global entertainment media market and information; have contributed to the changed nature of media management.

Electronic media organizations play an important role in democratic society. Beside, supplying the public with entertaining, informative and other kinds of 'products', electronic media organizations affect culture and help shaping social reality (McQuail, 1994). At the same time, they are an important element of the economic system. Economic performance of the medium is becoming an increasingly important area of study, since media policy cannot be limited to political and cultural values only. At any event, media policy is becoming an essential part of the economic strategy of the whole society, and the fact is that the role of media is becoming more and more involved in overall societal development. Economic rationale argues for the most cost-efficient media production. Concomitant with political, social and cultural welfare, the economic principle constitutes the fourth dimension of the mass media democratic functions (Van Cuilenburg and Slaa, 1993).

Taking into account the reconciliation of demands that various stakeholders impose on the media, i. e. the public (for information and entertainment), owners (for profit), advertisers (for accessibility) and society (for fulfilling public interest), management and administration of media has become a very complex process. Media are obliged to fulfil various interests and observe technological development, changes in regulation and social trends. Their critical role in society also makes their management (Žilič Fišer, 2010). With its powerful impact on the society, television is an important institution playing a central role in the functioning of modern democratic society, especially in the transfer of values. All these characteristics and peculiarities of the environment in which TV media operate make the study of their management rather complex since it has to address various areas of scientific research.

Market liberalism requires stricter performance criteria for public service institutions. In a market-oriented society crowded with private players tracking economic rationale and the highest possible cost-efficiency, transmission of such a rationale from the private to the public sector is a necessary trend. Mixing of private and public managerial practices requires setting appropriate standards for the functioning of a whole range of social services. From the viewpoint of television institutions, new management approaches are the answer to the challenges of the market: how to produce more with limited resources (production and programme capacities) in a heavily competitive market. The most essential demand imposed on the management of television institutions over the most recent period is the imperative for cost-efficient performance, involving not only economic efficiency but also operational and organizational[1] efficiency. This demand is a consequence of the new competitive environment in which TV broadcasting services operate.

The book deals with the unique role of the television medium, coupled with the unique position of television organizations in the social system. TV broadcasters operate in a social environment marked by specific political, economic and cultural pressures. Therefore, we present different media systems and their response to the environmental challenges. In this book, the evaluation model for accessing performance and efficiency output of the managerial process combines traditional and economic measures of research.

The chosen method of research is a case study exploring different dimensions of the British public service commercial TV broadcaster Channel 4 and the Slovenian public service TV broadcaster RTV Slovenija. Operational efficiency refers to the productivity of organizational units and the quality of products; organizational efficiency identifies the organizational capability to respond to the changes in the environment.

The central research question how to manage conflicts of interests arises from the study of a hybrid – a public service and commercial broadcasting system. The purpose of this book is to study the managerial processes in a television system that operates in the public interest and at the same time pursues economic efficiency. Another challenge is to define possible approaches to bridge conflicts between the interests of the special social mission and financial efficiency. This book aims to contribute to the theory and practice of media management in

1 Operational efficiency refers to the productivity of business units and the quality of products; organizational efficiency refers to the organizational flexibility in responding to social changes.

general, in particular television, as well as to the wider field of communication policy.

The milestones for the study of media management are the target objectives of media organization as presented by the model. The study focus is on three key forces that drive performance of media organizations: politics, economy and technology.

The area of **politics is studied with concern for the public interest** being the cornerstone of media performance and justification for their existence in the society. In the area of **economics, investigation focuses on economic efficiency,** which enables media organizations to survive in the media market. In the field of **technology, the study of technological acceptability** of media organizations deals with the convergence and technological acceptability of a medium operating in the multimedia society.

Objectives of the Study

The primary purpose of this book is to present and critically evaluate different approaches and methods for improving the efficiency and effectiveness of television organizations' performance, with particular emphasis on the public service media systems as the key element of the European media service.

Objectives set at the beginning of the topic under research are:

- to define the role and significance of television organizations in society
- to present the significance and methods of media organizations
- to present the peculiarities of media economics and management characteristics of television organizations
- to identify various television systems and determine challenges and tensions arising inside and outside national television systems
- to set criteria for the study of performance output in television organizations, point out and explain the significance of engaged performance in the marketplace, and ensure economic efficiency in public service TV broadcasters
- to present results of the analysis of the management performance output in a hybrid, public service and commercial broadcasting system, as well as to critically evaluate management strategies of the corporation under research.

The study seeks to make general claims about the performance and effects of broadcasting management based on systematic and objective observation of television organizations and other relevant factors. It also traces the phenomenon how public-service commercial television systems perform in and respond to the social environment, and examines the complexity of the managerial process in television organizations. The book however does not identify and study management process marked by the conflicts of interests, fulfilment of public mission or economic efficiency in television organizations.

In the study of mass media, media systems and management and administration processes, the starting point is the supposition that the emergence of television relates to its unique mission of public good, which the economic rationale for profit should also accept and observe. Observance of the public good and a unique social mission do not bar organizations from an engaged performance in the market and economic efficiency. That is why management of television systems requires reconciliation between two contradictory yet compatible objectives: the fulfilment of the special social mission and achievement of economic efficiency

The starting point of the study in this book is the claim: *Successful performance of a public service medium (in this case of television organizations) needs observance of both of the two objectives: the mission of public good and economic efficiency, which is an imperative for surviving in the dynamic liberalized media market. The solution for achieving the ultimate target is to use modern management approaches.*

The research topics deal with only part of the media system, precisely with the organization of the public television service. The main reasons are that public broadcasting services are still key players in the European media market and rapid changes in society impose additional managerial tasks upon public broadcasting services.

TV broadcasting services are the most popular targets of criticism because of their great social impact, integration in economic and political social systems of their national environments, and because of their role in providing for the public good. The most common complaints are about their rigidity; that is why they appear to be the most interesting case studies to examine how they apply principles for entrepreneurial success. Additionally, the commercialization and a crowded media market, as well as mixing of private and public managerial practices, require the setting of more appropriate standards for the operation of a large number of social services.

The commercial media sector is not subject to demands for fulfilling public interest. Consequently, frictions between the public and economic interests are not so obvious. Moreover, their instruments of incorporation are also economy-oriented and they finance themselves only by commercial resources. Examination of transparent conflicts of interests in the media market is possible only by the study of the public and commercial broadcasting sector. In the corporation studied, the conflict of interests is also transferred inside the system, which requires the application of mixed managerial practices.

The literature on theory available in the field of television organizations management is rather small. Particularities of the case reviewed required investigation of how commercial and public media systems function and addressing of the areas of political, administrative, communication and economic dimensions of media.

The model of the television organization chosen for the case study is unique. The primary research method used enables precise comprehension of different categories and their interrelations. The information and knowledge gathered will answer the research questions posed. The study will set criteria to evaluate the efficiency of the television organization and its management. Besides this, the applicability of different management approaches will be tested on the study case of the public-service broadcaster RTV Slovenija.

Data for this study derive from different sources. They include interviews with key people from the broadcasting industry in Great Britain and Channel 4, short interviews with key employees in the television organization, and analysis of the vast majority of data gathered from different sources. These are the Broadcasting Acts of 1990 and 1996, the complementary analyses and information of the Department for Culture, Media and Sport. The data also derive from the documents of Independent Television Commission (ITC), reviews of studies and annual reports by ITC and Channel 4 from 1982 onwards, Provisions for frequencies from 1993 and 1998, statistical data by the Broadcasting Audience Research Board (BARB) and ITC. There were also helpful academic debates on the British broadcasting system and the studied TV station, as well as many of publications on Channel 4. The purpose of surveying the multitude of different sources was to shape a historical framework, describe specific essential issues and events in a particular period, and prepare starting-points for interviews.

Credit for the research framework enabling detailed study and insight into an internal media organization that is usually hardly accessible is due to yearlong collecting of data and periodically interviewing of key British broadcasters, media regulatory authorities (study trip) and research work in the London University of Westminster. Finally yet importantly is also the author's work experience gained as head of a production unit in the public service TV broadcaster RTV Slovenija and in the mainstream commercial TV station.

Documented records served for drawing up a useful skeleton of events; however, they did not comprise any descriptions of essential motivational forces or crucial aspects of the Channel 4 performance. Interviews with key persons were therefore critical to fill in the missing details. They helped put the events into a broader context and bringing to life historical events. As such, they form the primary research material in this study. A large part of the research thus focuses on the interviews of persons being or having been key decision-makers in the British broadcasting industry. Together with the research into the hybrid media model, the model of the public-service broadcaster in Slovenija was also explored. RTV Slovenija as the only public-service TV broadcaster in the country, and at the same time the only public TV broadcasting service that underwent the transition and social change (and is still involved in the structuring process), is a case studied on criteria believed to be relevant for the managerial process. Media organization in Slovenia confronts many challenges originating from complex political, economic and technological circumstances. However, there exists potential for introducing a model to restore managerial standards that can generate development impacts in the environment in which it operates. The work and research experience in RTV Slovenija account for a different and in-depth insight into the topics of media management based on on-site work and relevant issues.

Why a case study of a hybrid model of broadcasting

In the 1950s, the first commercial TV station came on air in Great Britain, which also meant the beginning of commercial broadcasting in Europe. In the 1980s, a new media player, Channel 4 came into operation in the dual media market. Channel 4 pioneered a new model of broadcasting organization contrasting with the existing public and commercial broadcasting models.

The environment in which Channel 4 began its operations differed entirely from media remits in other countries. The only commercial TV broadcaster, ITV, did not compete in advertising with the BBC because it was subject to a strict regulatory regime, and in terms of programme contents, it was complementary to the public-service television. Comparison between the British environment of that time and the Slovenian (or another European) environment today evidences at least three key distinctions. They are: 1) there are more competing players in the market; 2) they at least partially compete with the public service television for advertising share; 3) they subject to a much looser regulatory regime, and are less restricted concerning management compared to the first British commercial television.

The reason for choosing Channel 4 for the case study is its unique position and status in the British media market as a hybrid (commercial and public service) managerial system. While the dual media system with public-service broadcasters on one side and commercial broadcasters on the other dominates in Europe, Channel 4 operates as a hybrid model of broadcasting merging features of systems, the public-service and commercial. The nature of a television institution fulfilling both public service and economic objectives assumes mixing of managerial practices used in public service institutions and those used in commercial systems. Challenges of such a type of organization are coordination and eventual reconciliation of conflicts arising between the interests of a unique social mission and commercial efficiency. Its outcomes indicate the chance of survival of the mixed management approach in Europe. Public-service broadcasters in Europe faced with the need for redefining their role and strategies for fulfilling their public and commercial objectives can take Channel 4 as an example model for their future development.

Since this book aims to study management practices in TV organization from different viewpoints and looks for the features of successful management approaches, it seemed reasonable to choose a model with different managerial characteristics that are used both in the commercial and public service systems. Channel 4, which exercises a special mission as a public-service broadcaster and operates as a commercial broadcaster at the same time, proves to be an excellent model for the study of management in television organization and for solving existing social contradictions between the public interest and market-oriented efficiency. Channel 4 was founded by the state to exercise a special social mission. At the same time, its performance exclusively depends on its economic efficiency, since market revenues are the sole source of its financing. It is treated as a commercial, public broadcasting service.

The dynamic media market featuring economic, technological and political changes causes changes in the role of the public service and commercial broadcasters' management systems too. As a hybrid model of broadcasting operating in the dual media market, Channel 4 has made a step forward in adapting to a media market that is constantly changing and it is expected to change even more in the future. With its approach, it solves the dilemma between public and profit-oriented interests by treating the public television as a business system.

The central objective of this case study is to give a detailed historical perspective how the concept of the Channel 4 broadcasting model came into being, and research its performance. This study involves analyses of key corporate politics, strategies and "cultural" decisions as well as their implications for the identity and management of Channel 4. Furthermore, the study aims to evaluate the efficiency of Channel 4 in terms of not only financial performance but also its contribution to cultural and political developments in Great Britain.

In addition to the media organization analysis, the environment in which it operates and interacts shall be described and examined. For this reason, we present its compatibility with economic and cultural policies of society as well as how they affect each other. Economic and political pressures, as well as cultural pressures, create an institutional context for the media organization. Such pressures, together with the environment, put a seal of uniqueness on this broadcasting model.

The results obtained from the study of the Channel 4 management will help to answer the question how the corporation examined bridges conflicts of interests in exercising the mission of public interest and economic efficiency. Successful management approaches and strategies discovered by the study could be a useful tool for public-service broadcasters to cope with economic, organizational and performance inefficiency. A reasonable choice to study the applicability of the Channel 4 management approaches and strategies was the public-service model of RTV Slovenija. RTV Slovenija has undergone various political, economic and social changes, and furthermore, the same model of public-service broadcasting is in force in other parts of Central and Eastern Europe.

The study of the media organization consists of three mutually connected segments depending one on another. The environment structure is defined within the framework of media systems. Management is explored in the chapter Management of Organizations. For the study of media performance efficiency, a framework called assessment of media output was set. It consists of economic and political criteria, which enables definition of the efficiency of management strategies in the case study.

The case study is the Channel 4 media organization, which has been explored in terms of all three segments over a period of five years: the media environment, management strategies and performance output. The basic research model whereby media organization is explored, and which indicates levels on which media organization is studied, is an adaptation of McQuail's model (1992: 87) featuring three key characteristics: market structure (environment), management methods and performance output. *Environment* denotes essential characteristics of financing, control of the medium, competition, market dynamics and limitations. In this way, the regulatory regime and limitations of Channel 4 together with the functioning of competition will be described. *Management* refers to the adopted managerial practices that define the production and programme contents strategy, advertising strategy and concern for innovation. The study presents the programme and marketing strategies of Channel 4 in these respects. *Performance output* comprises key elements needed for the evaluation of the functioning of the media organization. They refer to efficiency, quality of products and developments. Performance output standards comprising traditional and economic criteria enable the presentation of particular quantitative data needed to evaluate the performance of a chosen television organization.

Figure 1: Process of the study of the media organization

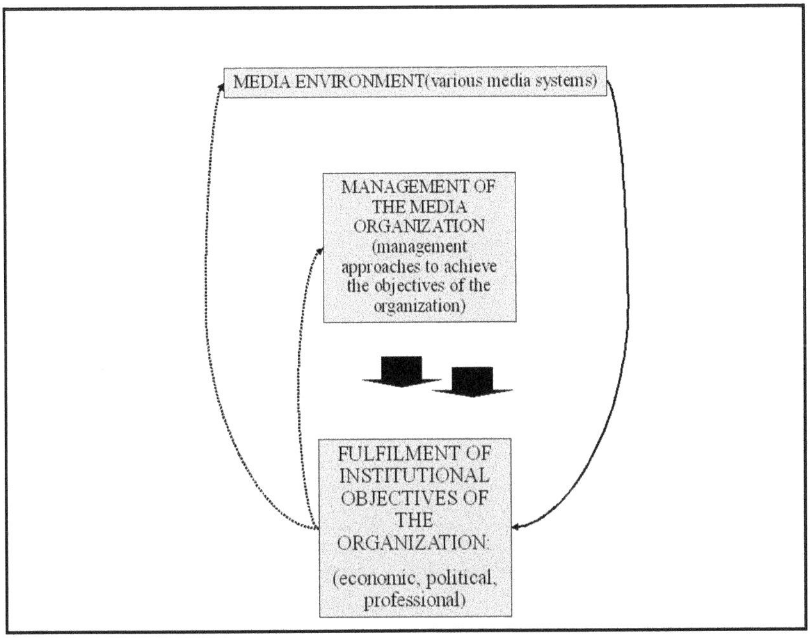

The following chapters aim to expose the performance of media systems, primarily focusing on television since it influences social changes and substantially contributes to overall societal development.

2. Media Organization in Society

This chapter presents the communication concept and the role of media in society as the central mass communicators. The complex role of media, especially public-service television, requires a broad-range theoretical basis that addresses various areas of science. An understanding of television as a political and economic force serves as the cornerstone for defining frameworks of successful television management.

Mass media play an important role in social change and participate in the creation of social reality. Interpretation of events creates "secondary" events. Social change perceived after a time is, however, the result of how the events are understood (as per media interpretation) and not merely of the events themselves. An undeniable fact is thus that mass media play a critical role in the creation of our reality today and tomorrow.

In comparing mass media, it is evident that they have different strengths of impact on the audience. Television evidences the most powerful impact in transmitting political information. Television is the essential source of information on social developments for the majority of the population. Television participates in the process of social change: it is at the same time a creator and a product of the social change. Such a study of the social issues raises many questions about its role in shaping changes in society, and not merely reflecting them.

The growing influence of the TV broadcasting medium has also caused a change in its definition. Television "output" ceased to be merely a "mirror" to society. Instead, it is defined as a precise selection of interpretations of events (Hoggart, 1976: 18). Television frames the world for the people to live and understand it more easily, experiencing it as if real.

Television is one of the elemental political and ideological institutions in society. Its wide range of activities comprises setting priorities in dealing with events, contributing to the enforcement of cultural norms, and perhaps most crucially its activity in relation to "those who rule dominant institutions" (Gitlin, 1980:10). Inasmuch as broadcasting media do not merely reflect a reached consensus or given "reality", but tend to select and reproduce the definitions of the "reality" as being benevolent, and even justify them, they contribute to the process of "legitimacy" and "the shaping of a consensus".

Relations among television, politicians, and the state are marked by compromises and conformism on either side – television and political players. Today, the means for expressing dissatisfaction or implementing censorship can differ from those in the past; however, primary motives and triggers have remained the same. In addition, there is no assurance that they will change in the future either (Splichal, 1992: 60).

The line between the moment when a chance of influencing a large group appears, and the moment when this valuable chance usurps a certain group of people can hardly be defined. Bourdieu (1991: 171) asserts that the emergence of new political elite is due to the shaping of firm positions by political players. The strength of positions closely relates to the control of key social institutions. The national broadcaster is one of those key social institutions. All of this gives new political players a rather stable position and enables them to manoeuvre successfully in the political arena.

Mass media that express values and characteristics of society on behalf of which they operate cannot exist as entirely independent of the social system. Hence, stratification and relations of power are also expressed in institutions such as mass media. Supporting the ruling values can (usually) mean also supporting particular ruling groups.

The study reveals a clear connection between the stratification system in society and the mass media communication process. This interconnection is demonstrated in the following principle: Higher social status in society means higher social and economic power, and thus easier access to the mass media and control of the communication process. Access to the mass medium usually represents an expression of power in all societies.

The functioning of mass media inclines more towards maintaining the existing power groups than calling them into question. Media institutions are supposed to function in harmony with other institutions and support prevailing society's norms and values.[2] In a society facing serious internal conflicts, it can happen that individual segment groups of the national medium take different viewpoints. In a democratic society however, the medium is expected to keep away from the conflict and take no point of view. This is typical for television, being additionally controlled by the public watchdogs and thus forced to observe an adequate level of neutrality. Neutrality is encouraged because it gives television a chance to respect, if not openly support, the existing regime, and at the same time to reject radical changes. This also means that the ruling groups co-shape media contents and decide what news is and which information is

2 The study concentrates on large television organizations. It aims not to extend the discussion to the alternative mass media respectively (TV stations) that are also big players in the social change, since they reflect the voice of groups opposing the prevailing norms and values.

the most important. The functioning of national media thus often reflects the functioning of the ruling political group, not because of its political stance but because it maintains social stability, and consequently the existing social order. Supporting dominant social elites and interests of the ruling mainstream is usually also the safest way for the institution itself to survive.

Mass Media

The term "mass media" refers to a means of communication functioning on a large scale with access to almost every individual in the society. It denotes various media operating in society – print, film, radio, television McQuail, 2001. Today, various new sorts of media emerge in the market, featuring more individuality and interactivity. Although the number of new media grows rapidly, there are only a few indicators showing a decline in »traditional« mass media. There are more signs, however, that they play a role in spreading the activities of the new media in the market and responding to the challenges. The importance of mass media still lies in their phenomenon of universality of access, high prevalence (popularity) and public character. All the characteristics of mass media reflect the functioning of political and cultural life in society (McQuail, 2001: 4). In relation to politics, mass media are gradually becoming:

- the essential element in the process of democratic politics by providing a communication field and channels for full discussion and dissemination of various information and standpoints;
- means to exercise power for those who have privileged access to the media (politicians and government representatives).

In relation to culture, mass media:

- shape the primary source of definition and impression of social reality and the expression of collective identity
- represent the most common form of leisure providing the largest shared cultural environment

The growing media industry is empowering media even more and strengthening them in the economic sense. McQuail (2001) asserts that it is rather hard to draw the line between media theories and societal theories, and defends the standpoint that media form a special social institution in society with its own rules. However, they are still simultaneously governed by the definitions and restrictions of society in general. Media are thus dependent on society despite their considerable independent power arising from their autonomous position and economic power. Between society and media, there exist various interconnections depending on the time and space media operate. McQuail (2001) lays stress on the different position and performance of media in different social systems.

The field of media theory embraces various perspectives. McQuail emphasizes different approaches between the left wing (progressive) and the right-wing (conservative) tendencies, which have significantly affected the creation of theories.

Media theories differ in their approach to creation, being either critical or more applicable. Critical theories try to draw attention to the problems and errors in media operation practice, relating them to social issues. Applied theories on the other hand focus on the communication process in order to solve actual problems, exploiting mass media more effectively in this way.

Theoretical approaches labelled as media-centric or sociocentric expose autonomy and the impact of communications. Media-centric theories lay stress on the autonomous performance of media and the enormous impact of mass communications; sociocentric theories, on the other hand, understand the media as a reflection of political and economic forces.

A theory is a systematic set of ideas that can help to comprehend certain phenomena, lead developments or forecast consequences. According to McQuail (2001), there are at least four types of theories crucial for the mass media communication. They are social scientific theory, normative theory, operative theory, and everyday theory.

Social scientific theories bring general statements on the nature, functioning, and impacts of mass media communications that are based on systematic and objective observation of the media and other relevant factors. The research body of this type of theories is extensive, as they address broad social issues in detailed aspects of individual information. Some scientific theories deal with the understanding of circumstances, a few of them with the development of critical observation and the rest of them with practical applications on the public information process.

The second type of theories is *normative theories* dealing with the study of circumstances and prescriptions of proper functioning in order to achieve desired social values. These theories play an important role in establishing and legitimizing media institutions and have a significant impact on expectations about media. A large part of the media research is the result of the intention to apply various social and cultural norms to the functioning of media. Normative media theories are not unbiased by themselves, however they can comprise objective research methods from the field of social science (McQuail, 1991).

The third type of theories is *operative theories*. They refer to a set of practical ideas that the media practitioners apply to their media work. Such an approach is a frequent practice in many professional organizations. Media organizations help a lot in the study of many issues, such as how to select news, how to satisfy the audience, how to advertise successfully, how to function within the requirements of socially tolerable conduct. In some points, operative theories overlap normative theories (for example journalism ethics).

Everyday or *common-sense theories* on media usage are, according to McQuail, the knowledge of behaviour gained through personal experience with the media. They enable the understanding of developments, how the media influence peoples' lives, how the audience follows various media categories etc. Using these theories enables the making of appropriate selections, developing patterns of behaviour, and determining the lifestyles and identity of the media users.

Functions of the media

Today, democratic functions are incorporated in many "western" media policies and shall be observed by each medium. Their examination dated back to the 19th century when the normative media theory was conceived.[3] Normative theories emphasize the concept of the "free market of ideas": *The main function of the media in a democratic society shall be a contribution to a free and open competition of ideas in the political process.* Freedom of speech, the press and expression, in other words, freedom of communication, occupies the primary position in liberal normative media theories.

Concerning the normative theory and recommendations by the defenders of mass media freedom, the media in modern democratic society are obliged as the intermediaries between politics and the public to meet three political or intermediary functions respectively.

The first function is informative: The media shall inform the public about political targets, governmental strategies, proposed plans and political changes. The informative function is the oldest among the primary media functions, being mostly a top-down process. In political reporting, the media serve as a communication channel leading from the top of politics (government, parliament, political parties, associations, and other institutions) to the voter base.

Besides the informative function, there are another two functions: the function of expression of and the function of control. The function of expression lays

3 Precisely: The origin of the normative theory dates back to the 17th century England when John Milton (1608–1674) wrote *Areopagitica* on censorship.

stress on the medium as a communication channel through which individuals or groups can express their views and pursue their political, cultural, and social identity. The function of control refers to the medium as a watchdog in society. Contrary to the informative function, the functions of expression and criticism are bottom-up functions directed from the voter base up to the top of politics.[4]

Functioning as the public watchdogs, the media also play a significant role in preserving the democratic principles of society. In their role as watchdogs, the media presumably also reduce the power of the ruling elite in a country (Curran, 1990:84).

The public watchdog function is actually a tool for protection, as it generally defines the role of a medium in terms of the government control, protection of the public and prevention the power holders from exceeding their powers. The role of the media as the public watchdog denotes an important role in public life, which is that of the fourth estate.[5] Based on that, the media are given an additional representative function, as they deal with proceedings reflecting the public interest (people). The representative role is demonstrated in the media's orientation towards catering to the interests of the broadest public, gaining its support, and enabling their own development, since their functioning is led by the market. In their representative function, media strategies today lean towards appealing to the broadest public, due to their profit-oriented logic.

In the past, the media could limit their functioning only to the fulfilment of the essential communication functions (of information, expression, and criticism). However, with the development of society, such a definition became too narrow. Commercialization of the media, in other words the profit-oriented representative function, especially in TV broadcasters, has become another characteristic and the fourth media function.

Commercialization of the broadcasting system demands a revision of the public broadcasting concept. Broadcasting forms an integral part of the market-based economy. Together with political and sociocultural welfare, communication technology can also contribute to the economic production of goods and services; hence, economic development depends more and more on communication techniques. The economic rationale of society calls for economy and the highest productivity possible, which are realized by adding the fourth economic dimension to the mass media democratic functions.

---

4 Based on the authors Van Cuilenburg and Slaa, attention was drawn to the three primary "political" functions: the informative function, the function of expression and the function of criticism.

5 The term "fourth estate" denotes adding the representative power to the three other branches of power: executive, legislative and judicial.

However, the principal media function remains the fulfilment of the public good and the public interest, which is explored in the following chapter.

Public interest in all media

The concept of the public interest and the public good, with reference to the mass media, means that the media are obliged to fulfil a large variety of important objectives in modern society and that they are generally expected to pursue their mission well. The concept of the »public interest« in political theory (McQuail, 2001) implies that the media function is based on particular rules and norms that prevail in society, especially in relation to justice, democracy, honesty and common social and cultural values. The idea of the public interest comprises both positive expectations and also specific restrictions and types of accountability.

Held (1970) describes two principal versions of what the public interest creates and how its content is defined. The "majority" perspective on media functioning tends to equate the public interest with "give the public what it wants", which satisfies the majority of users in the media market. The opposite view is "unitarian" or absolutist. According to the latter, the public interest is determined by one dominant value or ideology that leads to a paternalist system in which decisions on what is good are made by a group of professionals. Between the market-oriented version and the paternalist model of the public interest, there exist various alternatives; however, they offer no appropriate explanations.

The idea of the public interest often closely relates to a specific media form or structure, which is public-service broadcasting. In fact, the idea of the public interest in mass communications and public broadcasting institutions overlaps, since the latter are often considered as a principal contribution to the functioning of the social environment. The public interest demonstrates itself in universal access, services for minority groups, attention paid to national interests, identity, and culture, and demands for informative and educational services (Blumler, 1992). Equating the public interest with one type of media structure is however too narrow, since it denies the fact that the private media are also obliged to serve the public based on the public interest.

Hence, the media and the "public interest" need a broader examination than merely the functioning of public media, since the standards of the public interest can be applied to all the central media irrespective of their founders or ownership. Hoynes (2001) suggests four essential characteristics of media operating in the public interest:

1. *Diversity*
   In a democratic society, the media are obliged to present a broad variety of current views and experience.
2. *Innovation*
   Impressive technological potential and substantial investments in the media industry relate to creativity and innovation in form and contents. TV broadcasting develops cultural practices, encourages creativity and originality, and radiates the dynamics of society.
3. *Content* (quality)
   Entertainment is one of the essential imperatives of television programme contents; however, the media are also obliged to provide quality programmes and deal with key social issues.
4. *Autonomy*
   The media should provide citizens with information and views that do not depend on the centres of power in society (the ruling elite and financial centres of power), since media biased towards economic efficiency and ideology tend to reduce the perspectives they offer to the public.

Evaluation of media functioning based on the above-mentioned criteria often inclines towards subjective interpretations. The same danger arises in evaluating the "societal" role of a medium within the frameworks of standpoints that are frequently those of the elite. Drawing attention to the social role of the media does not mean a demand for narrow cultural and political media contents or supplying merely "unworthy" populist contents. The social role, which a medium is obliged to fulfil, defines the objectives for their functioning in terms of economic, social, and political paradigms.

The media performance is subject to free-market forces. Furthermore, the media product features some specifics (McQuail, 2001) that make media economics peculiar. A few economic features differentiate it from other industries. The media are hybrid institutions, as they operate in the market providing their products to the audience and services to advertisers; they are very critical about the type of the product they sell and the technology they use. The media business contains a high level of creativity and uncertainty. The uncertainty relates to the users' evaluation (it is still very difficult to predict the public reaction to certain products). Media products comprise a large share of creativity, which make them an artistic output. Media products have to change on an everyday basis; hence, their performance depends on a short response time. Today's media product loses its value in the future. The media naturally tend towards concentration.

Trends towards a monopoly position in the market are present all the time. Maybe, this is due to the advantages of monopoly control of advertising and great social power. The media differ from other industries since they provide for *social interest* and in particular a *mission of public good.*

Characteristics of media performance give the media a unique position as an important social institution.

Media institutions

Performance of media institutions reflects expectations of the entire public as well as of other social institutions (such as politics, government, religious communities, minority groups, legislation, economic sector). Media institutions have gradually developed around the key activities of publishing and dissemination of information and culture. Their performance often overlaps the functioning of other institutions, especially those dealing with public communication activities. Media institutions fall into different segments depending on the type of technology (print, film, television) and within each type often also geographically (the local print as compared to national print or television).

Besides, a number of other typical features are added to the core activity of the production or dissemination of knowledge (information, ideas, and culture) to the benefit of those who would want to communicate, being either individuals or the community. The main features are the following:

- A media institution is located in the "public sphere", which means that it is in principle open to all receivers and senders. The media deal with public affairs and are available to the public. They are accountable to the public for their performance (through legislation, regulation, and pressures by the state and society).
- Publishing and dissemination of information to all members of society also allow them to have a lot of freedom in economic, political, and cultural activities.
- Despite the fact that the media aim to achieve impact, a media institution formally holds no particular power. (There also exists a logical relationship between the absence of power and a high degree of freedom; the less the power of an institution is, the greater is its freedom in economic and political activities).
- Participation in a media institution is voluntary and imposes no social obligations.
- A medium is, by definition, organized professionally and bureaucratically.

- For their output, media organizations use creativity, in which however immeasurable performance criteria often prevail.
- With the development of technology, which is playing a growing role in the media industry, the technological sector introduces additional criteria in the use of media products.

The media industry for a long time used to be considered as a social institution, and not as an industry. Over the last decade, it became more of an industry. That is why understanding of the basic principles of media structure and dynamics is necessary, requiring examination at the economic, political science and sociocultural levels. Despite the fact that the media have arisen as a response to social, cultural, and political needs, they are mainly managed as business systems. The trend in this direction has even increased over the last decade, due to the growing industrial and economic importance of the entire information and communications sector.

The uniqueness of a media institution is also because its activities undoubtedly have an economic and political character too. These activities include the production of goods and services, which are often private (used for the distinct satisfaction of each person), and public (regarded as essential for the functioning of society as a whole).

This public character of the media stems mainly from the political function of the media in democratic society, and from the fact that information, culture and ideas represent a common asset. At the same time, their use does not reduce other people's ability to use them, as is the case with air or daylight (McQuail, 2002: 190).

The media have historically developed as the determining factors in public life. That is why there are various mechanisms for their promotion and operation in the *public interest*. Nevertheless, the media operate completely, or at least partly, according to the principle of the market economy.

It is not surprising that the wide variety of national and social environments does not offer any standard definition of media institutions (McQuail, 2002). There are several different perspectives for determining characteristics of media organizations. Tunstall (1991) applied the economic/industrial perspective, which treats the media as business systems. The critical political-economic theory provides concepts that stem from criticism of capitalism and refer to the processes of concentration and commercialism. The third perspective offers a study of media structures in relation to the public interest. The fourth perspective discusses media institutions from the internal or media professional point of view.

The media has the dilemma of acting between different social forces: *political, economic, artistic, and technological.* This is why the operation of media institutions relates to the political, economic, artistic, and technological realm in society, carrying also different expectations and performance criteria.

Performance of media policy

Modern analysts have studied the broadcasting system in different ways; in any event, it was difficult to differentiate business policy from television policy and television programming.

In studies of the broadcasting service, changes in its performance and in media policies in the context of market economy can be traced already in the 1970s. The study of television structure through indicators of economic development and market economy was critical in the early studies of this topic (Owen, 1979). There are also traces of examination about the importance of technology as an essential factor in broadcasting performance and media policies. The importance and efficiency of a medium related to the encouragement of technological development in society and its integration in a media organization (Forrester, 1985). Analysts in the 1980s focused on the study of the impact of ideology on the determination of media policies and operations of broadcasters. They stressed existing values in society as a key element in setting a baseline for the performance of media institutions (Negrine, 1988). New Marxists pointed up the impact of private ownership (Murdock, 1990), which was supposed to determine new media policies in Europe. One can also trace evidence of the study of sociology of media organizations (Tunstall, 1991), which enables the operation of the media industry in various dimensions. A new populism policy also emerged as an essential factor in the broadcasting performance, setting policies and their amendments (Dyson and Humphreys, 1990).

A study of a media system with a view to ensuring social values and realizing the social importance of the system represents a significant starting point for exploring and studying the broadcasting model of media system presented in this book. Reference criteria for the study of a modern media model comprise the specificity of media organizations, provision of social interest, importance of technology as an essential generator of the change process, and the market economy as a realm in which the system operates. Modern theory on the study of the media and their performance output uses different approaches to assessing operation and efficiency of the media.

In discussions about the mass media, assessment of performance output is frequently used; however, it lacks a clear and specified meaning. It can refer to various self-assessments in the media industry with the aim of attaining economic or production targets. It can be used for the evaluation of public policies of mass media (for example, in relation to a monopoly position or cultural standards). It can also be used for critical evaluation of many levels of operation and as examples of medium performance. Furthermore, it can be used for determining efficiency in informing, persuading, mobilizing, sales, and other issues.

In a market-oriented environment, the media are supposed to meet various demands concerning their role and significance in society, which was not the case even a decade ago. Their existence and operation were self-evident, as they gained a guaranteed position already with their foundation. Today, it is different. The public media seek for their competitive advantages and complementarities in relation to the private ones. Their policies aim at facilitating the balance between their operation and reconciliation of all their objectives.

Competition is growing in relation to the products that the company offers, and its users accept. Television measures its competitive advantage primarily by the programme contents. Undoubtedly, the quantity and share of viewing are the measures of success; however, viewing is only one of the competitive criteria. Individual programmes and the entire offer of programme contents are measured by the following criteria: quality, innovation, professionalism, standards, social relevance, and service to various interests. All of these criteria, being not purely economic, determine performance benchmarks and the competitive advantages of players in media market.

Broadcasting and aspects of the study

The study of television as a unique social institution requires mining at the various social levels where television operates and from which it receives impacts on its activities.

Broadcasting requires ongoing examination at different interrelated social levels. Broadcasting associates with the following aspects of study in the first place:

- Economic aspect addresses economic science.
- Political aspect uses political science.
- Content/editorial aspect relies on sociocultural science.
- The technological aspect mines from technology.

All the aspects require different research methods. Porter (2003) emphasizes broadcasting as a very complex area for research, being organic activity that needs to be studied at different levels. At the same time, it is very important to examine the nature of relationships between different aspects.

Broadcasting differentiates from other economic activities because it is subject to the following hypotheses (Porter, 2003):

- rarity of sources requires precise control and regulation of a broadcasting organization;[6]
- management of the national cultural policy through the central broadcasting organization (it is assumed that television is a »parastatal institution« that enables management of the national cultural policy of the country, and is itself a part of the national cultural policy at the same time);
- an impact by broadcasting on the performance and thinking of individuals about society and life. (Treatise on the influence on the thinking and acting of individuals derived from the approach »uses and gratifications«, according to which the public perceives media contents with regard to their needs.) Porter adds that the ranking of events is more powerful than the content itself, which makes television an exceptionally powerful institution in society.

Research on broadcasting at the economic level

Assumptions by A. Smith justifying the functioning of economic factors do not apply to broadcasting. Firstly, users are supposed to have power and knowledge about the prices and products. Secondly, if you produce more you can produce more cheaply. Broadcasting[7] is a specific activity for which particular economic assumptions do not apply. However, some areas of research can be studied at the economic level. They are:

- payment of *radio frequency fees* (national and international pricing of radio frequencies);
- broadcast licences (costs of using radio frequency spectrum, problems with determining what comprises "state aid", the state's requirements about programme contents);
- sources of financing (defining the type of income: subscription, advertising, sponsorship, paid contents);
- exclusion of programme contents from the transmitting infrastructure;

---

6 An assumption of the rarity of resources is hardly justifiable nowadays because of satellite and cable television channels that do not need "state-protected" frequency spectrum for broadcasting.

7 A broadcasting organization wants to sell information; however, the users do not want it until they know what they are buying. That is why parliament (government) acts as an intermediate link working to the benefit of the public – users – by defining the functioning of media organizations.

- convergence of broadcasting and telecommunications;
- the issue of universality of service broadcasting.

In listing the topics that require exploration at an economic level, their political implications are also examined. It is therefore difficult to separate research at the economic level and that at the political level, because this issue requires a more extensive examination and a multidisciplinary approach. The fundamental question of when broadcasting ceases to be a television and becomes just an economic-oriented industry requires solving at various levels.

Research on broadcasting at the political level

Television is treated as a political force; hence, discussions about television are becoming increasingly political issues. The fundamental question in exploring a central television institution in society is certainly a question how to determine the functioning of a public television service, which closely relates to a political environment.

The study of various areas of broadcasting at the political level requires an examination of:

- what makes broadcasting a public service
- the issue of universality of services
- freedom of speech
- facilitating competition in the broadcasting market

Questions about television as a public service are always open at the political level. Furthermore, discussions studied at the economic level often require study at the political level too. All decisions, however, address the scope of monitoring and regulation, which is always a political issue in society.

Research on broadcasting at the cultural level

At the cultural level, the primary questions concerning broadcasting policy deal with editorial (programming) performance:

- What constitutes a programme of a public service broadcaster?
- Is public television obliged to support film industry?
- What is the central liaison in society between the national culture and the broadcasting sector?

The topics examined at a cultural level are also addressed at political level, which contains all mechanisms for the monitoring and regulation of the broadcasting sector.

Research at the technological level

Television as a medium has undergone various changes over time. During the period of convergence with other platforms, television has been gaining a different and more complex role. Technological acceptability asks questions about the scope of digital literacy and about how to bridge the digital gap generated by the lightning speed of technological development. Television as a medium and a media institution should take account of the changed competencies of users who, as digital natives and multiskilled users, are ready for a different perception of media products.

Basic questions asked at a technological level concern acceptability of media products with regard to the modified use of the media:

- Does a television product take account of the changed time dimension as television contents gain in size due to faster platforms?
- Does media production take account of the transformation of the users?
- Does the convergence with other media take place at different levels?

Stress is laid on the complexity of the study of broadcasting and television itself, since television is closely integrated, as a system and institution, with the social system in which it operates. In particular, activities of public television are part of activities, values, and norms of the overall socio-political system.

Complementary role of public-service broadcasters

The term *public broadcaster* in the United States means a corporation that is in the minority; viewers and listeners finance it on a voluntary basis, as it facilitates particular cultural norms. In many countries, especially in Western Europe, public broadcasters are established by law and are usually financed by public resources (often by subscription fees). The common objective of their operation expresses the need to serve the public interest and provide for essential communication needs in society.

There exists no commonly accepted theory of a public-service broadcaster; hence, individual national societies evidence different ways for achieving the general objective of public television. Guidelines for the operation of the BBC, often presented as an ideal public television model, date back to the year 1922 when defined by John Reith.[8] His guiding principles for the functioning of an overall public broadcasting system[9] still apply: »**inform, educate, and entertain**«.

---

8 John Reith was the first Director General of the new BBC.

9 Today, they are commonly valid guidelines for the public service – not only for the BBC.

The general development of audiovisual media over recent years, and the expansion of media markets (both global and national), have caused a crisis in the institution, which has been operating for decades with various trade-offs.

The main weakness of "public-service broadcaster" derives from two types of tension. The first tension arises between the necessary independence and accountability for the financial resources received. The second tension is between the attainment of the objectives that society defines as a public interest and the fulfilment of the requirements by the public as users in a broad media market. Without objectives for the public interest, there is no way for a public broadcasting service to continue to exist. However, the public broadcasting service cannot achieve its goals without the public.

Contrary to private, market-oriented broadcasters, a public TV institution observes the norms of the social system from which it originates. The type of its management classifies it as a public institution (public sector); it was also established as such. Blumler (1992: 213) emphasizes that in any event, there is a close relationship between all forms of television and the social system.

Specifics of a broadcaster as a socio-political institution also reflect its special organizational structure. The complementary role of public media derives from their particular position in society, which enables wider dimensions of success compared to an economy-driven efficiency. However, there is a risk of a smaller level of viewing, but it is also supposed that they would contribute to the success[10] of the entire system in another way. That means that the lower-rated programmes are supposed to be as crucial for the success and value of the production as the high-rated ones.

The strength of public media force in competing with private media is in offering a motley mix of complementary programmes. Complementary programmes reflecting variety, peculiarity and competitiveness enable public television to consolidate its market position and ensure its survival. In shaping a successful strategy, it is critical to find the right balance between an appeal to broad tastes and focusing on a narrow but crucial public. Therefore, a new task of a public broadcasting service is finding a balance between qualitative and quantitative advantages of its programme contents.

This balance also allows it to determine priorities of programme contents, which is the main difference in comparison with commercial broadcasters.

---

10 This success is recorded by cultural and political criteria. The programmes that reinforce social values and norms, as well as play a strong educational role are strengthening reputation of television organizations and substantially contributing to the development of entire television system.

The prioritizing of programmes by a public-service broadcaster does not mean merely providing specific contents that commercial broadcasters do not offer. Excluding certain genres from the public broadcasting programme would mean enclosing it in the moulds of minority interests. In principle, it is reasonable for the public-service broadcaster to foster all kinds of programmes and genres that may, however, differ from its commercial rivals, since it pays more attention to the quality standards.

Setting priorities based on target audiences assumes that a commercial television focuses only on programmes for the general public while public-service broadcaster shall serve the minorities' interests as well. This assumption has many inherent contradictions and denies the necessary role of public television as a representative of the interests of society in general too. This assumption also denies interests of most viewers and the mission of the public-service broadcaster to operate for the public good.

The criteria of target audiences is so broad that it should perform both of the two roles – public broadcasting service as a "cultural forum" addressing a society's minority, and public broadcasting service as a co-designer of cultural development. Coordination of both roles requires coordination between different target audiences, which means that public media operate both in the interests of the minority and the majority in society.

The third criterion of *qualitative priorities* (Blumler, 1992: 208) is the one that allows a public-service broadcaster to be different, providing for the public good and adapting to all public audiences at the same time. Qualitative priorities differ from a commercial broadcaster by their particular characteristics and not by the programmes, functionality, standards, and quality. Qualitative criteria and responsiveness to the public needs are the priorities that ensure "competitive advantage"[11] in relation to other players in broadcasting market.

This book's purpose is to present a media organization and evaluate its functioning based on criteria concerning satisfaction of the public good and economic performance. Due to the special role of the media in society, qualitative and quantitative priorities should be observed to meet the objectives of the media management process. Broadcasting is studied from a variety of perspectives that define the position of a medium in society within the context of its social mission.

This chapter presents the position and the role of mass media in relation to the social environment in which they operate. The position of a mass medium

11 Economic terms used in this book seem reasonable also for specific uneconomic phenomena.

demonstrates its institutional character as it also acts as an important social institution. The essence of a media institution's complex character is that its activities are undoubtedly economic and political too. These activities include the production of goods and services that are often private (the use for distinct satisfaction of each person) and public (regarded as essential for the functioning of society as a whole). This public character of the media stems mainly from the political function of the media in democratic society, and from the fact that information, culture and ideas form a common asset.

The debate on broadcasting is also a political issue since broadcasting is understood as a political force. It is therefore difficult to separate research at an economic level from that at a political level, because these issues require examination that is more extensive and a multidisciplinary approach. Exploration of television always associates with explorations at political, economic, technological, and cultural level. Demarcation between different levels in such a dynamic institution is ineffective because it cannot answer all of the complex research questions.

Broadcasting is an important social institution that acquired the special task of meeting a social mission. Operation of television is expressed by its media structure, which tracks various organizational objectives and copes with different social tensions during its management process. Coordination of the social interest and market orientation is certainly an essential tension in a media organization, leading to the conflicts of interests at the social and institutional level.

An important task of each television organization, both public and private, is delivering economic prosperity and taking account of an economic rationale.

3. Management of Media Organization

This chapter deals with different dimensions of media organization management. The transfer of successful managerial practices from the private to the public sector is an important approach used by modern media organizations. Media management is distinctive also in ethical dilemmas that are obvious also in television organizations.

Any organized community of people (organization) needs to be constantly administered and managed, regardless of its formal structure (private or public corporation, institution, association) or its size and the socio-political arrangement in which it operates and develops. This fact has never been disputed. However, most of those who have studied organizational issues from a scientific or political point of view paid most attention to the analysis and content of two primary organizational functions, that is, management and administration of organizations in concrete political and economic circumstances. Studies of management and administration date back to the golden age of classical scientific management, to the time of the development and use of classical administrative management, and the period of bureaucratic and organizational models based on behavioural science. They also continued at the time of the emergence of modern organizational structures based on the system theory, cybernetics, logistics, ergonomics, sociology, psychology, praxeology, information theory, and computer technology (Albarran, 2002; Pringle, 1999; Anželj, 2002).

There exist various definitions of management. For the study of management in electronic media, Pringle (1999: 3) uses a definition that describes management as »the process of planning, organizing, influencing and monitoring to achieve organizational goals through coordinated use of human and material resources".

The literature on organizations offers several definitions and detailed interpretations of management and administration, and a few insights into interconnection and interdependence between these two subjects.

The dynamic nature of electronic media requires their management be a process that includes all the necessary elements to reach the objectives of their business policy. However, it was not always considered as a dynamic process.

Modern theories on the organization's management

An organizational system consists of people, money, assets, equipment, and data arranged in a way to realize the company's targeted goals. Organizations carry out similar activities including input resources (work, capital, and equipment), production process (transformation of input resources into products or output items), and output elements – products, goods, services. Feedback on input resources and production processes helps decide whether anything needs to be improved or changed to achieve targeted objectives. The role of management is to coordinate the input, the process and the output elements, and to analyze and respond to the results. Hence, the system approach to management involves examination of the external environment and assessment of feedback in order to identify changes and meet objectives.

Administrative management steers the work process in administrative bodies or their organizational units by exercising managerial methods at each activity. These managerial methods help to understand the essence of management activity and to access the character of individual administrative tasks. Hence, it is necessary to divide the task into different jobs and work operations if necessary, and analyze each part of the process with regard to the managerial methods used.

However, fundamental misunderstandings about managerial process are quite frequent, considering management to be a domain of top managers and focused only on the organization's highest level. The fact is that managerial processes should perform at all organizational levels (this is the case also with electronic media) because different organizational units pursue different goals, which all accomplish the primary corporate goal (Kraut et al, 1989). Most organizations, and electronic media, evidence at least three management levels.

- First management level: First-level managers supervise the work process and report to the next management level (in television organization, the head of the news department reports to the programme director at the middle management level).
- Middle management level: Middle-level managers are responsible for the implementation of common objectives, which are crucial for the corporate goal (middle management levels in TV organizations are, for instance, marketing departments, programming sections or television techniques departments).
- Top management level: Top-level managers carry out organization-wide monitoring and leadership, determine internal and external factors that affect the functioning of the organization (the managing director coordinates and reconciles operations taking account of internal and external factors).

Management of a media organization depends largely on its local, national, and global environment (Žilič Fišer, 2007). Several factors affect management and operation of media organizations.

- Holders of broadcasting licences bear a significant responsibility. The holder (temporary owner) of a broadcasting licence can be a small local television station with national coverage. The licensee is responsible for its activities to the licensing authority. As with investors and owners in other industries, here too the special motive of the holder of the licence has a key role in the management of the television.[12]
- TV stations are competing in both the media and advertising markets. This competition closely relates to audience reach, which is essential for business success. Paying attention competitors' activities and reacting to them are integral parts of each media organization's business and programme strategy.
- Government exerts its powers on TV industry activities through executive, legislative, and legal authorities. The media regulatory framework, brought into force by media legislation (the mass media act and the public broadcasting act) affects managerial strategies within organizations, and their activities in the market. Media organizations respond to the state regulatory policies by restructuring and grouping of companies.
- The global space reflects in the operation of the media industry, which produces a global product. Harmonization of various international agreements enabled the emergence of new markets. A number of giant media players are penetrating the markets outside the United States, Western Europe, and Japan, and localizing their products. Media corporations too, competing with services, contents, and goods in the global market bring about globalization of media in the 21st century.
- The availability of human resources in a community, particularly the creative sector, can put extraordinary pressure on media management and activities.
- The key factor that influences the management of media organizations is the general public, which is the driving force of television programmes.
- In the commercial broadcasting sector, commercial advertisers are generators of change as they resource activities and programmes of TV stations. Their activities and changes in the advertising market substantially affect the broadcasters' managerial process.
- Economic situation in national and global markets affects broadcasters' businesses and programmes, since they depend on the revenues from commercial advertising. Advertising budgets in flourishing times are higher than during

12 Contrary to other industries, owners in the media industry are often interested not only in the profit but also in other kinds of welfare (social and political impact for example).

an economic recession. In the case of public funding, activities also depend on the country's economic situation, since the government fixes licence fees relevant to the country's economic indicators.

- Professional standards set for operations in the media market, and especially in the broadcasting sector, give a distinctive character to the managerial process in TV organizations. Journalistic codes of ethics and media product standards are also signs of the special nature of TV products and services.
- Technological development has enabled the birth and development of radio and television. Electronic media are dependent on technological advances, since they influence their production, distribution, and broadcasting of media products. The essential principle of today's managerial process in media organizations has become the observance of all technological changes.
- Societal factors play a deciding role, since broadcasters ought to fulfil the community's interests and provide for the public good. TV organizations ought to respond to the trends in proportion to the size and structure of the community and social groups. Each community tends to change not only with regard to demography but also owing to technological and global forces. Today's usage of media featuring simultaneous functions and synergic effects of various platforms is much different and more personally experienced than a decade before.
- Users' requirements arising from a different use of the media impose new demands on production and indirectly on management too.

Environment of media organizations consists of a large number of interacting and interdependable factors that affect their management. Technological, regulatory, political, global and social trends have brought changes to the whole media industry. Changes in TV's managerial processes are responses to the turbulent media market that requires observation of all influencing factors.

Success of media organization

If we transfer the findings to the management of television organizations, striving to attract their target audience and provide for the public good and at the same time ensuring cost-effective usage of resources, we encounter the fundamental dilemma that challenges TV's managerial processes. Attracting target audiences with quality programme contents is one of the goals. However, it is vital to achieve also economic efficiency to ensure for a TV broadcaster to successfully operate and fulfil its mission in the media market.

Players in the media market are forced constantly to search for mechanisms to adapt to the changing environment, and to balance different interests. It is evident that the media environment is rather complex. Each of these relations affects the decisions taken by the management; moreover, the internal environment also requires coordination of different objectives.

Block (2001: 208) points out fundamental paradoxes of the management of electronic media:

- *Balancing creativity with the control of projects*
  Media services require high creativity to make a successful product (service). Making a creative media product or service often requires much freedom, but control of the project hinders it.
- *Managing the chaotic and unstable media market*
  Many external changes and contradictory effects from the community condition media management.
- *Observing both the changes and the constantly growing obligations which these changes bring with them*
  Taking account of changes and being a step ahead imposes great obligations and additional costs on the organization.
- *Dealing with the ever-changing technological platform*
  Technological changes determine development trends of the media industry, which is liable to incorporate its business and social mission in its technological development.

Management of public sector

Most of the public institutions are facing the requirement for increased efficiency and flexibility due to the constantly changing environment. These requirements derive in particular from the growing complexity of society and the environment and their interactions. Moreover, they are also due to the evolution of public sector, and thereby the increased need for coordination, participation and decentralisation, but above all they is due to the scarcity of resources. Demands for reduction of expenditure and for procurement of new sources of revenue require effective approaches to management, administration and operation. It also requires the development of monitoring systems for steering operations and assessing performance efficiency.

One of the responses to these demands is also introducing principles of *new public sector management.* The term new public sector management or new public management denotes the concept (Žurga, 1997) that suggests transferring positive managerial and operational practices from the private sector to modern public (administrative) bodies. These elements relate mainly to the economy and business economics, methodologies and approaches to management and administration, working methods and techniques, organizational structures, entrepreneurial mindset and action. The new public sector management also emphasises a people-oriented approach, both towards users and employees. In respect of the organization's mission and business strategy, it defines the products/services provided, determines an appropriate organizational structure to serve this purpose end, and introduces new approaches, working methods and entrepreneurial thinking by employees, which all contributes to the building of a new organizational culture.

Introducing principles of new public management involves a modern arrangement of work processes, demarcation of responsibilities and powers – particularly in terms of accountability for results – an increase in the autonomy of the organization and individuals, and trends towards a flat organizational structure. The mission steers the organization's operations to achieve its goals and determine its efficiency and effectiveness.

Introducing the principles of new public management also means shifting from the mindset of "operation on the safe side of the law" (Huijegevoort, 1994) towards an efficient and effective operation in order to achieve the targeted objectives.

New public management primarily consists of the following elements:

- *Outcome-driven orientation*
  Orientation towards outcomes focuses on the definition of a product or service that is a result of individual process, and answers the question what an organization and/or its unit will do or provide. Besides that, the definition of products or services relates to the definitions of how to achieve and measure results and how to define accountability for them.

- *Customer-driven orientation*
  Orientation towards customers means striving to meet users' expectations and carrying out their orders with quality and timeliness. A customer-oriented approach requires a different organization of work processes, which may affect organizational structure too. Organizational structure should be flexible enough[13] to respond more efficiently and rapidly to environment changes and to ensure constant change management. The degree of an organization's flexibility depends on how strong the impact of the environment is and how urgently the organization needs to respond to environment changes.

---

13 Delivering a high-quality media product or service means taking account of the interests and wishes of the public, and flexibility in responding to changed media usage.

- *Restructuring work processes*
  Work process means a sequence of activities that should be carried out to achieve a particular target. Activities that organizations should carry out to improve their work processes consist of examining and analysing current work processes, defining positive elements, preparing options to improve the work process and implementing the agreed changes. Improving work processes is a permanent task.
- *New organizational structure and new management methods*
  Restructured business units and modern management modes can be leveraged to enable flexible responses to changes in the external and internal environment.
- *Introducing new work methods and restructuring the workplace*
  Changes in organizational structure induce restructuring of workplaces, which often requires implementing new work methods too. Restructuring processes do not focus only on the targets for increased efficiency of work processes and customer satisfaction, but also those for increased satisfaction of employees with their work (and their output), which requires restructuring of individual workplaces.
- *Increasing efficiency and effectiveness*
  A new structure of work process (processes) can at least improve performance output, simplify the work process, and enlarge efficiency of individual workplaces, which can result in lower production costs and greater customer satisfaction.
- *Delegation and autonomy*
  Wherever possible, delegation and transfer of decision-making competences to the employees who contribute directly to the value chain of individual processes is a usual practice. Communication among individual autonomous units and within them becomes horizontal in terms of cooperation and coordination, contrary to the previous vertical-oriented practice. Such an increase in powers encourages employees to adopt a more entrepreneurial way of thinking and stimulates their motivation to express their human potentials and creativity.[14]

14 TV product is a fruit of creative activity, which has greater significance than in other industries. Original performance and creative potential produce more excellent results in a relaxed and non-authoritarian relationship.

- *Outsourcing*
  Individual activities or even whole work processes, if appropriate and cost-effective, can be outsourced to reduce costs or to gain specialist knowledge that the organization itself does not provide. Such a practice is useful particularly in TV production, since hiring external production associates is more rational than maintaining a large production base within the TV house.
- *Defining and delimiting responsibilities*
  Specifying obligations and responsibilities of each of the units or individuals is necessary to achieve a rapidly responsive and flexible work process. Taking responsibility also contributes to the employees' affiliation with their organization, and to the building of organizational culture.
- *Creating competitiveness*
  Competitiveness inside and outside the organization reflects the striving to maximize the services and products provided.

Public versus private sector

Political and administrative theories have intensively examined differences between the public and private sector since the mid-19th century.[15] Private sector and consultancy companies often advocate the view that the differences between the public and private sectors are not essential. However in the public sector advocates that the public and private sectors are different. According to the latter, the fundamental difference is the impact of politics and providing for the public interest that is characteristic for public sector (but not for private).

Drucker (1999) sees efficiency as an essential difference between the private sector and non-profit organizations. Business circles usually define efficiency only in financial terms, which is too narrow, but on the other hand very specific and concrete. The non-profit sector does not possess such a simple criterion; its only argument is that the public sector serves the public good and provides for the public interest. This, of course, is not enough; it is necessary to provide mechanisms to check whether the funds have been used in a way to achieve the planned results and that the organization's performance can be considered as efficient.

Economists spotlight two essential groups of characteristics that differentiate productions of public and private sectors: organizational and individual incentives (Ferfila, 1994: 90–93). Organizational incentives are not relevant in the public sector because there is no possibility of bankruptcy. Moreover, there is no

15 J. S. Mill: *On liberty* (1859).

competition in the public sector, which commonly urges managers to achieve efficient performance and prudent management. Such reward mechanisms and dismissal policy lower motivation of individual employees. By creating public policies, the public sector, can directly or indirectly, intentionally or unintentionally, affect private-sector activities (Ferfila, 1994: 13–14). Government has a coercive power that the private sector does not have, but in general, it can create its work processes alone. The difference between private and public institutions is also in the way they appoint executives.

A tendency towards the convergence of public and private sectors is also evident as a necessary consequence of their interdependence. The management of non-profit organizations experiences transformations from bureaucratic administration towards business management, deregulation, and emergence of free-market regulation instead of non-liberal planning regulation. Further convergence of public and private spheres is evident in many areas. Most recently, a so-called public-private partnership[16] has been developing by integration of the two sectors, which bridges the limited ability of public sector to invest on one hand, and increases the competitiveness of the private sector on the other hand (Ferfila, 1994).

The public and private sector also differ by their organizational cultures. They demonstrate differences in attitude towards the environment and fundamental missions (observance of legality or making a profit). The activity of the public sector is based on providing for the public good, while the private sector gears toward measurable indicators to target profit.

Due to the fundamental missions of each sector, it is not reasonable to apply the entire philosophy of one sector to the other. Hence, it is obvious to take into account the different targeting orientations of both sectors arising from the current position of the mixed economy – the coexistence of private and public sectors, and their mutual interpenetration, integration and interdependence (Ferfila, 1994: 13–14). It is also necessary to review how each sector operates, in order to decide competently to what extent business principles could be applied to public sector management.

Organizational culture is the basis for change management at the managerial and employee levels, and in relation to the public perception of the organization. Corporate culture reflects all the changes and trends of an organization that takes care of its overall development and observes trends in the environment to find its own competitive advantages.

16 The so-called *public-private partnership* attracts attention from many authors nowadays.

Public and commercial TV stations have different organizational cultures by virtue of their primary missions, which require change management and adaptation to the rapidly changing media market.

Media organization

Theoretical studies of media organization require observation of various relations and relationships inside and outside the organization. Relationships often mean interactions and interchanges, sometimes also conflicts with the community and individual actors within the organization. Gebner (1964) describes mass communicators being under pressure from various stakeholders (such as commercial advertisers), competitors (other media), governing authorities (legislative and political pressure), professionals, other institutions, and the public.

Taking account of such approaches, TV broadcasters can be placed in a situation in which they have to confront various restrictions and demands relating to their power and influence. A TV broadcaster forced to manage at least three inherent professional groups (administrative, technical, expert), also has to deal with economic and socio-political pressure.

However, pressures and claims do not necessarily hinder media organizations from performing their mission. Some pressures balance the others (e.g. public support against the pressure of commercial advertisers, or media prestige against external institutional pressure). Absence of external pressure could point to social marginality and unimportance.

Media organizations make relationship most often with:

- community (target: public good)
- owners (profit)
- pressure groups (different social interests)
- general public (quality programme)
- advertisers (accessibility)
- internal public (various professional matters)
- the governing groups (meeting the role and funding framework of public TV service)

Comparing the goals that a media organization pursues, they usually contradict one another. On one hand, there is an obligation to track material goals (financial), and on the other hand to fulfil immeasurable values. That is why most television broadcasters are managed as "businesses", yet track ideal goals. At this point, the question arises who the "users" of these ideal goals are. Is it the whole of society or just a particular group of customers (commercial advertisers)? Are they the owners, the audience, or the employees of the organization? Whose goals do they follow? There is no single answer to these questions. Evidently, organizations have a variety of potential users, whose aims and wishes they try to fulfil and satisfy. Tunstall (1971) describes media organizational goals in economic terms, distinguishing them between revenue and non-revenue goals. The non-revenue goals refer to purposes without direct financial aspect, such as gaining prestige, exercising power in society, or achieving some normative end, for instance serving the community. Revenue goals are of two kinds: gaining profit from direct sales to consumers (payable platforms) and from selling advertising space. Serving the public interest (audience) is a basis for the fulfilment of all the mentioned goals, since a television organization acquires its power from sufficient public support. At the same time, the public interest also results in the acquisition of advertising revenue.

Each media organization has to cope with inherent tensions between the goals of social interest and the goals of market-oriented rationale. Various authors express different views on TV's priorities in their studies.

Dilemmas of broadcasting policy

Although the book deals mainly with the management of TV organization, it is impossible to separate business policy from broadcasting policy and programming. The TV business strategy closely relates to programme guidelines. However, the capability of an organization to design programme guidelines vitally depends on various socio-political dilemmas in its media remit.

Television organizations look for the structures to observe all the changes in the media environment. Deregulation, new technologies, changes in societal perspective, and growing competitiveness have levered changes in the broadcasting market. The broadcasting strategic objective is searching for tools to respond adequately to complex changes: convergence, digitisation, channel monitoring, new regulatory frameworks, and a massive increase in the number of channels resulting in fierce competition. User options have increased, and the vision of many channels in the national broadcasting system overshadowed the paradigm of public broadcasting service. A question arises whether there is an audience in democratic societies or merely consumers in the market.

With market competition, affecting broadcasting systems more and more evidently, the dilemma between competition and quality has become obvious. Quality within the context of the broadcasting system is only a matter of subjective perception. The growing competition has produced a wider range of products and services than ever before. However, it is a big question whether we can talk about a real diversity. There seem to be more possibilities, however a multitude of channels does not necessarily bring diversity, and it could happen that all the channels would offer the same contents. The same types of broadcast contents and even the same broadcasts are disseminated on different channels, since production is smaller than distribution. The decline in programme standards raises numerous questions. Many argue for the thesis that the quality is dictated by the audience, since they equate quality with the delight of the audience when they get what they want. The taste is dictated to some extent by the society's culture. If the culture shapes the customer's taste, and if the market determines the culture, than the market can fulfil all the needs and wishes it has generated by it. The magic circle is closed when we realize that our taste is influenced by what we see, and shaped by what we are offered (Kung-Shankleman 2000: 215).

In the managerial process of television organizations, dilemmas arise on at least three levels (Kung-Shankleman 2000). Firstly, how to define TV organization: as part of social infrastructure and an important social institution, or as a player in a free market? Secondly, how to define the audience: as citizens of a democratic society, or merely as consumers in the market? Thirdly, is it true that programme diversity reduces with the increase of competition, or does the competition incite programme diversity? A fourth definition could be: shall traditional television production adapt to the use of other platforms (internet, mobile devices) or keep its strong position as a traditional TV channel?

The management of television organizations requires different approaches because of their basic social mission and organizational culture.

Broadcasting policy consists of cultural values that a television organization pursues: the corporate mission, the nature of competition, the audience, relations between competition and quality – all of which determine the organization's products, performance, and strategic decisions.

Dilemmas in the management of television organizations are of the essence in seeking the appropriate theoretical management model. Scarcity of studies on the management of public television organization requires exploration and use of theoretical contributions from other fields.

Management of a public service broadcaster

General theories on organizations and management applicable to media organizations are very helpful for study the management of public-service broadcasters. The theory on public service media organizations can consist of theoretical contributions from other fields, as for instance the theories on professional organizations, non-profit organizations, and political management. All these theories provide an important contribution to the understanding of management in public media organizations.

The understanding, however, is not complete if the study concentrates only on the organization of media contents, since reviewing merely editorial policy and professional programme standpoints cannot provide precise analysis of the media organization. What is essential is the management approach, and that should be observed at all levels when studying the media organization.

Piccard (1989) points out the concept and the role of the market, consumers, production issues and the market's responses, as well as market structures and their relations to capital markets. In his studies, he also pays much attention to government intervention in the market, analysing how the government promotes societal goals, and exerts decisive leverage over the management of media organizations by regulation and control.

Alexander, Owers, and Carveth (1993) pay attention to various industries, such as print, publishing, television, film, advertising, and present an analysis of the global integration of the media industry. Gershon (2000) pays particular attention to the activities in the community and to the developing of strategies. He also studies the growth and expansion of media companies into transnational media corporations.

Researches into the media management (Lavine and Wackman 1988, Lacy et al. 1993) put an emphasis on a few factors that differentiate media from other industries: the nature of a product, the type of employees, particular organizational factors in media organizations, and the unique role of the media in society.[17] Lavine and Wackman can see the challenge for media managers in reconciling two goals: producing media products with limited resources, and producing innovative and high quality contents (messages). The analysis refers to the U. S. media market again. Owners are primarily interested in earning profit from their investment. Employees want reasonable pay, and the audience requires an appropriate (cost-effective) product or service in exchange for the time and money they spend on it. The basic source of revenues for media organizations is advertising; therefore, managers aim to "sell" the audience to commercial advertisers. In some media management analyses, the idea of merging profit with social responsibility is evident.

The media management theory is based on the idea that media organizations operate in two separate markets: in the advertising market and in the consumer market. McManus (1994), however, added another two decisive markets: the capital market and the resource market.

---

17 The book emphasizes a unique status of media organizations as the only business entities protected by the First Amendment of the U. S. Constitution, and also other regulatory characteristics that media institution observe, such as copyrights, the right of privacy and integrity, libel.

The study of the management history of the Swedish broadcasting corporation (Tjernström, 2002) reveals that traditional literature on media economics and management offers very few appropriate theoretical concepts for the analysis of management in the public media organizations. To find relevant theoretical concepts, a number of analogies should be observed. He also states that public service media organizations operate in two separate "markets", precisely in two separate environments – in the consumers' environment (audience) and the politicians' environment setting the rules of play.

Tjernström, 2002 bases his studies on the theories of management control that appear relevant for various fields in the media and communication research: the information-brain theory, the work process theory, and the agency theory (Tjernström, 2002: 243).

Analysis of a public-service TV institution should focus not only on the management control or journalistic professionalism but also on organizational goals. The primary management role in public media organizations is often on the side of professional journalists – those who speak in favour of essential values and broadcasting goals (Blumler, 1992), and often oppose the owners' or their representatives' wishes.[18] In addition to the aforementioned theoretical frameworks, which we try to apply to the management of broadcasting, it is important to highlight the theories that contribute to the studies of how a public broadcasting service operates. Studies on political management offer some relevant theories, and theories on non-profit organizations can help too. These theories are replacing traditional management objectives for efficiency with objectives for legitimacy and the integrity needed in management. It is important to search for appropriate theoretical approaches that comprise studies on the management of media organizations, and take account of three essential management principles: the commercial, political, and moral.

Theories on political management assume that organizations operate in a technical environment (consumers /users market) and an institutional environment. Standards of structures, processes, and ideologies can serve the purpose depending on how much they contribute to the overall effectiveness and how much attention they pay to different missions. However, it is hard to find a

18 One of the reasons for greater support of professional and cultural standards in public-service TV management lies in the setting of managerial preferences. Namely, executive directors of public-service TV broadcasters in Europe often come from the journalistic sector while people with economic preferences more often manage commercial broadcasters (economic experience and knowledge). Professional journalists in public-service TV broadcasters are also a strong driving power (trade unions).

guarantee that the requirements of the political environment contribute to the desired models of organizational behaviour. It is most likely that it is not easy to merge different requirements and aspirations to one primary goal of conducting an efficient production process. There exists a conflict between efficiency of achieving the owners' requirements and efficiency of the production process.

More specifically, there is a remarkable friction between institutional demands and the requirement to pursue efficient organization. At the same time, it is obvious that various public-service units track different objectives. Furthermore, disagreements over achieving various objectives also exist at the corporate level and among organizational units. Different owners (shareholders) have various interests, expectations, and ideologies towards public services, and thereby different aspirations towards management structures and processes.

To overcome such tendencies, organizations use different strategies that often contradict one another. Managers can seek mutual interests among the owners' aspirations; however, the relation of powers among the owners and ideological frictions represent extraordinary obstacles to efficient management. The situation described significantly differentiates from the efficient management as presented by the literature on traditional management. Although the management focuses on rational behaviour, political management theorists expose another kind of rationality that does not track efficient production so much, but replaces it with "legitimacy".

At the same time, it is natural that the organization develops a strategy containing contradictory elements when it accepts different requirements from the environment. Different groups within an organization identify themselves with different requirements, some of them with informative roles, the other with providing for entertainment and attracting an audience (viewers). Conflicts between goals, the structure, and external perspectives merely reflect the environment in which the organization operates. This theory focus differs from that which the agency theory observes. The latter concentrates only on conflicts among different organizational levels while a political organization also has to cope with conflicts at the same level.

Political organization deals with various ideologies and exists as a body that takes decisions and deals more with problems rather than solutions. The organization tends to be more general and less specific, but this also creates inefficiency. A public company that wants to meet various contradictory goals is similar to a manufacturing company that produces and supplies products for different markets. In both cases, costs of production are much higher.

Theories on political management may be very helpful in the exploration of public enterprises (Tjernström, 2002). Public organizations, such as public service broadcasters in Europe, are active in the political market since they pursue public needs and requirements. TV broadcasters' operators have different ideas about corporate goals; they track various ideologies and act in the political market, which plays a significant role in the market of public good.

Research into non-profit organizations has brought many helpful hypotheses to analyze the management of public media organizations. The necessary issues in these surveys are the questions of how to create incentives for efficiency of these organizations, which the ownership and management of which are not profit-oriented, and how to reconcile society's requirements at the same time (Oster, 1994).

Non-profit organizations are usually active in the areas where it is difficult to evaluate products and services, where a great ideological impact is obvious, where trust and responsibility are necessary, or where production in the public sector exists as an alternative. Non-profit organizations are typically labour-intensive and often based on a different form of funding. At the same time, non-profit organizations often have complex ownership structure, resulting in obvious contradictory demands on management.

Certain assumptions are relevant for public media organization, and it appears that a consideration of theories on political and non-profit organizations offers a significant understanding of public television. A public media corporation is often an extremely powerful player in the political field and a key player in determining national media policy.

Many media organizations act as commercial players, competing in the market with other organizations, and fighting for the audience's time and consumption. Their goal is to achieve the viewers' loyalty and profit. Important elements in this respect are advertising revenue, programme costs and employee costs. Media organizations, especially public services, are often a political project and subject to political orientation. Moreover, a media organization is often a moral project too. It actively cooperates in society and contributes to a particular social atmosphere. It interprets pictures as values and principles, trying to show its audience the world from the desired perspective. It strengthens confidence, authority, loyalty, and habits however from the position of power.

A media organization is a company acting in three fields: business, politics, and morality, which all influence the primary product of a media company – information. Commercial forces track sensationalism and glorification.

A media company tries to replace institutions that have acted to fulfil the right to be informed (news), the obligation to education (schools), and the need to be informed about the other parts of the world.

Various theoretical concepts make it possible to identify the starting points for European broadcasting. Theoretical concepts of political and non-profit management, moral theory, agency theory, brain theory, and the work process theory provide parallels with the research in public service broadcasting management. This makes it possible to contribute to the explanation of phenomena and reconciliation of management goals of the public broadcasting organization.

Ethics in media management

In the management process, it is necessary to take decisions that are not merely a routine, but address the scope of values and ethical behaviour. Ethics deals with key issues of what is right and what is wrong, and includes the character and behaviour of individuals and institutions. (Jaska and Pritchard, 1994). Day (2000) defines ethics as a branch of philosophy that deals with the moral aspects of life.

Ethics reflects social norms about what is morally right and what is not. On an individual basis, ethics enables proper understanding of behaviour, which is based on the principles and rules relevant for an individual. There exists no universally accepted code of ethics in the electronic media. Every organization can adopt its own code of ethics. Everywhere, where a group or corporate code of ethics exists, there appears a conflict between the corporate approach and the individual's moral belief. Various organizational units observe different rules. The top-level management in a media organization concentrates on the balancing of market needs (owners and other competitors), and on providing for the public interest.

Hosmer (1991) points out that those ethical problems and their solutions are complex processes. Decision-making is a complex process influenced by many factors. Many decisions affect other within the organization and the wider society, and have far-reaching consequences. It is necessary to consider many different options that are available; the lack of time, which is present constantly in TV management, makes a detailed analysis of each alternative impossible. Ethically sensitive decisions produce advantages and disadvantages, which one must deal with. Management decisions are rarely clear-cut and no-risk and their overall consequences are rarely foreseeable. Ethically sensitive decisions driven by values, standpoints and individuals' personal characteristics co-create a media product.

In the media management, there are key areas involving ethically sensitive decisions.

Serving the public and the market

A natural conflict arises between the media aspiration to serve the public and the market simultaneously (McManus, 1992). TV organizations have a special mission of serving the public interest, even though the rules and definitions on what the public interest is are not entirely clear. Therefore, media organizations and their management are bound to define what the public interest is. Despite traditional criteria (determining quotas and programme broadcasts), the public service is a highly imprecise definition, and each media organization bears the responsibility to choose how to realize this commitment. A period of deregulation has brought more freedom for this kind of decision-making, and the critics of deregulation point out that media do not care for the public interests anymore.

TV organizations are accountable to their owners and founders for ensuring a profitable operation. Companies in the media industry, like in other industries, are interested in making profit. An ethical dilemma arises when business interests prevail over other commitments (Day, 2000).

Dilemmas about the content programme

In the media management process, ethical issues often appear in relation to a programme as the most visible and obvious activity of the media companies. Most of the polemics relate to the broadcasts with controversial contents: violence, pornography, with a lot of controversy about the contents of children's programmes. Dilemmas over a programme can cause a conflict between the employee's personal belief and the corporate orientation.

Similarly to the conflict between simultaneously satisfying public needs and the market, a conflict arises also between the responsibilities for the programme (media industry) and economic pressures. Some of the most common conflicts are the problem of truth and accuracy, the right to privacy, conflict of interests (paid and unpaid contents), the confidentiality of sources and advertisers' pressures.

Ethics in advertising

Employees in marketing departments cope with many dilemmas and ethical issues. They bear responsibility to the general public (users), to the moral principles of individuals, competitors, advertisers, and businesses.

The importance of ethics and ethical decision-making in public television are particularly salient, due to its complex managing process, which requires taking many decisions that affect the scope of values and ethical behaviour.

Different approaches in management theories denote different schools: classical, behavioural, and modern school; all of them however have significant limitations in their applicability to the media industry. The classical school focuses on production and offers a useful understanding of management functions and roles. The behavioural school makes an important contribution by highlighting the employees' needs and their respective motivations. Modern approaches take account of the management process and management efficiency paying attention to the interdependence of the media and other social systems.

The changing nature of the communication industry rules out the possibility of implementing a universal managerial practice in electronic media organizations. Complex challenges that media have to face daily require individual analysis of each managerial operation, depending on their organizational structure, the features of the media market, market position, quality characteristics and organizational culture. In all cases, the fact is that management is a process consisting of a set of activities taking place alongside a number of other internal and external changes. The changing nature of a medium makes it impossible to use only general theory but requires selecting the most appropriate approach from all the three schools.

In the search for a theoretical framework to analyse the media management, especially of public television, it is essential to observe different theoretical approaches that contribute to the quality analysis. The theoretical perspective of agency theory, the theory of work processes and the brain centre theory were helpful in understanding the operation and relationships within television organization. Theoretical starting points for political management and management of non-profit organizations are exceptionally helpful and useful.

Management of a television institution has to confront a number of dilemmas that often require ethically sensitive decisions. The media industry bears various responsibilities: towards its mission and goals, the public, owners, their profession and society. Those kinds of dilemmas make the managerial process complex. However, the most challenging dilemma is how to fulfil public and economic interests at the same time.

Exploration of the public TV management addresses the fields of political science and administration, while the search for appropriate models for achieving corporate goals brings in economic and communication disciplines. Hence, this books deals with various social science disciplines as the result of the unique nature of media organizations and their dynamic management.

4. Broadcasting Systems

The present chapter tries to describe a real situation and the operation of the media system, and to present the many challenges and obstacles confronting the media market. A TV organization is an integral part of the political and economic environment, as well as of the political and cultural environment, featuring the culture, traditions, political system, democratic tradition and openness of each national market. Hence, advocating a single valid media model would be inappropriate. Among the given social circumstances, we shall highlight common characteristics applicable on the territories of the United States and Europe. Typical characteristics of the media operation and the environment in the US make up a free market-driven commercial broadcasting system. We also take into account specific characteristics of the European environment, which tracks the creation of a dual media system and tends to give the primary role to public broadcasting service.

Commercial dependency and minimal state regulation of electronic media in the United States proves that the broadcasting industry there is treated like any other industry or company whose primary goal is profit. In the United States, public broadcasting service too must observe an efficiency rationale.

The chapter focuses mainly on the functioning of the European dual broadcasting system. Here, public-service broadcasters have to compete with commercial players, which impose additional free-market rules on their management teams.

In the British media system, public-service broadcaster plays the principal role. The free market rationale is also quite important, which offers great opportunities to commercial players. The new, more light-touch media regulation, and a high degree of self-regulation give an even more decisive role to the free-market rationale. Channel 4 is a typical example of a hybrid television model combining characteristics of both public and commercial media institutions. Coordination of both tensions – free market-driven functioning and the unique social mission of public TV service – is clearly expressed in the Channel Four Television Corporation. Its special role in the market is also due to particular historical, political, and cultural circumstances, which stimulated the foundation of such a broadcasting model. European public TV stations undergoing transformation with an obvious identity crisis can find a solution for their further development in a hybrid television model.

The system in the national environment is influenced by central national and transnational TV corporations, which lead developments in the media market in accordance with the circumstances in the micro and macro community.

Public-service broadcasters have faced commercial media competitors in different periods. The programme policy of European commercial competitors has changed the media policy of public televisions. The television environment has changed with the advent of commercial actors and their influence on the advertising market, programme providers, infrastructure-service providers, and government legislative measures.

Various political, economic, cultural, and democratic rationales have encouraged the development of predominant TV models. In Europe, there prevails the public television model that operates in an environment with an increasing number of commercial players. The United States, however, feature the predominant role of commercial TV stations, while public-service players occupy only a small niche.

Commercial dependency and light-touch state regulation in the US

In the United States, market economics, constitutional democracy and freedom of speech are formally guaranteed by the Constitution. In 1791, shortly after the 13 member states ratified the Constitution, 10 amendments known as the Bill of Rights were adopted. The First Amendment prevents state control over the media: Congress must not adopt any act that would limit freedom of speech or the press.

The Communication Act of 1934, with amendments, provisions and rules, and the Anti-trust Act are the cornerstones of broadcasting policy (Cantor, 1985). Despite a large choice and the very fragmented ownership structure of the media, the U.S. audiences watch the news and entertainment programmes mainly of few corporations. These corporations are profit-driven businesses. They are also divisions of large corporate conglomerates. Despite the fact that they have emerged from TV companies, they are organized and managed like most other American corporations.

In the United States, the radio and later the television have retained the same mission and motives as at their emergence. A private company was established and it started promoting and using the radio's influence for advertising purposes.

Initial motives are satisfied when the radio or television reaches the maximum audience. If a mass medium intends to maximise its market share, it must avoid exclusion from any part of the population. The programme must be acceptable to the majority of the population. Furthermore, if it tends to be accepted by a large number of viewers, it should be as apolitical as possible (Gurevitch, 1994).

In the U. S. media market, where public television has not so many viewers as commercial broadcasters, there are strong arguments in favour of the free media market and the abolition of subscription-funded television.

In contrast to supporters of the European public TV system, libertarian theory advocates a media system free of any state control and without a public TV network (Bouckaert, 1994). Libertarians see one sole option for the existence of television (and radio): both shall be treated exactly the same as books and print! Libertarians, as proponents of the U. S. Constitution, believe that the government should refrain from in all intervention in the mass media (Rothbard, 1994: 99).

The U. S. critics of European media policy target at many points. They claim that it does not encourage innovation and economic efficiency and that it restricts individuals' freedom of choice without any reasonable need. They argue that the market is the only criterion necessary to rely on, since no government can successfully predict what interests such a diverse audience.

The U. S. TV Broadcasting industry is unique by its being treated like any other industry or profit-oriented company, while in many other states, electronic media are controlled (or even owned) by the Government. Most of electronic media regulation is based on economic grounds, because it protects particular economic interests. The capital structure determines who controls broadcasters in the United States, and determines topics and the rationale of programme broadcasting. The only difference is with public television stations that are not only profit-driven, but must also make a business strategy to provide them with sufficient financial resources. Even public TV stations must sometimes compete with commercial corporations in purchasing and sales of programmes.

Commercial TV stations

The U.S. broadcasting industry produces two primary products (Budd et al., 1999). First, it provides television programmes despite the fact that the majority of television production originates from a small number of studios in Hollywood. Besides programme production, a lucrative business is also the distribution of programmes through the sales and rentals of contents directly to viewers (video, DVD). Secondly, it generates viewers or, more precisely, it attracts the attention of millions of viewers. TV corporations gain masses of viewers by means of programmes for which advertisers are willing to pay a reasonable price. The value of these viewers depends on their quantity and composition, since viewers are treated as potential consumers. Therefore, products, programmes and viewers (as the primary objective) are all essential for the operation of the broadcasting industry in the United States.

The TV industry's heyday started in the late 1940s, when radio strengthened its advertising role. Pay radio services also increased. TV broadcasters also used this model until the 1970s, when pay cable channels started emerging. Today, we can talk about two economic models of commercial television in the United States: the traditional model of advertising-supported TV and pay-TV (Budd et al., 1999).

In American society, the number of TV channels has increased over the recent years due to the pay channels seeking their niche in the audience. Despite technological, political, economic, and cultural change since the adoption of the Constitution, the fundamental premise of the commercial television (the central medium in the U.S.) has remained the same – to make a profit.

TV corporations developed soon after the radio industry had blossomed. Three large corporations – ABC, CBS, and NBC soon acquired TV stations, which had been founded earlier to form the basis for the operation of the corporate TV broadcasting network. These stations, owned and controlled by corporate TV networks, are the most profitable TV broadcasters in the world.

An important feature of the US: commercial TV system is the separation of ownership from the control over programme production and distribution, which is the TV networks' domain. Subsidiaries or TV stations leave the central editorial policy to TV networks, which supply them with programme contents and lease advertising space. Hence, TV networks bear the programme responsibility and the right to revenues.

An important turning point for the operation of national television networks was the Telecommunications Act (1996) that increased the corporations' remit from 25 to 35 percent. This meant that TV corporations could acquire even more TV stations. January 2000, when America Online announced the takeover of the Time Warner, denotes the beginning of the integration of Internet and traditional media companies.

The U. S. commercial TV industry consists of a multitude of TV stations broadcasting 24 hours a day seven days a week.[19] It is the No. 1 player in the free media market; bound only by anti-trust law it sets management strategies that track only one, profit-oriented objective.

19 According to the ratings of 1999 (Albarran 2002: 8), the average household in the United States watches TV 7 hours a day.

Public broadcasting service in the US

In order to shed light on management issues, a great deal of attention is also paid to the concept and operation of the public TV in the US, although commercial TV dominates in American media society.

Non-commercial educational broadcasting reaches approximately 16 percent of all radio stations and 23 per cent of all TV stations in the United States. The public-service broadcaster constitutes one category within the non-commercial broadcasting service that operates under the standards of the Corporation of Public Broadcasting (CPB). A public broadcaster is a specialized field of broadcasting with unique concepts and principles. In contrast to commercial broadcasters, it does not focus on optimizing viewing ratings (targeting as broad an audience as possible), but on cumulative weekly viewing. The reason is the fact that it bridges programme gaps for the narrow-target groups, which cannot find space on commercial broadcasters. The public broadcaster's strategic objective is, therefore, providing programmes for minority groups and meeting as many different minority interests as possible in a week. Fulfilling an educational mission is also important, since such programmes mainly address disadvantaged groups in society, such as children and the elderly. The key difference between commercial and public broadcasters remains the sources of funding.

The U. S. management models of commercial and public broadcasting are similar. Commercial TV stations operate in order to make a profit; their managements use rational strategies that take account of investing only in programmes that attract advertisers. Public TV stations are non-profit by nature; however, they must justify their costs to ensure further revenues in the future, so their business ought to be extremely rational. This became vitally important in recent years, when government funding decreased. Therefore, rational management is the mainstay of both TV models.

The current public broadcasting structure originates from 1967, when the Carnegie Commission report on educational television was issued (Pringle et al., 1999). In the same year, most of the directives for the operation of non-commercial educational broadcasting came into force under the Broadcasting Act, which also gave the basis for the establishment of the Corporation of Public Broadcasting (CPB). In 1970, the CPB and some non-commercial stations established associations of public TV stations and radio stations called Public Broadcasting System (PBS) and National Public Radio (NPR). The associations provide affiliated stations with a variety of programmes and services.

The result of developments in the 1970s is non-commercial broadcasting, which operates at three levels:

1. Local non-commercial educational radio and TV stations, which are licensed by the Federal Communications Commission
2. Corporation for Public Broadcasting (CPB)
3. PBS and NPR, member corporations

In the late 1990s, there operate 368 non-commercial TV stations, of which there are 172 licensed and 349 operational.[20] There are four categories of licensees for broadcasting:

- Local communities – they found non-profit corporations that manage TV stations. This is the largest group of licensees for broadcasting, which is, however, very dependent on their communities' support.
- Universities – they carry on their educational mission via TV programmes (also by sponsorships).
- Local authorities – broadcasts act as an extended educational tool that functions mainly under the auspices of the State's schools.
- State agencies – they manage the largest number of non-commercial TV stations in the United States.

The size and structure of a TV station depend on the size of the market, the type of the broadcasting licence and the programme offered. Some stations also act as production centres and sell programme contents to other corporate members.

By the mid-90's, the basic funding of public stations comes from government sources, regardless of the user's non-commercial license (as mentioned above). In the last period, however, the primary managerial priority is to provide sufficient funding, as the Government's financial support was cut or in some places even suppressed.

Public TV stations are looking for resources to finance their programme since they cannot sell advertising space due to their non-commercial status. Main sources of funding are as follows (CPB *Annual Report 1997)*:

- The basic funding source for the majority of public TV stations is the Community Service Grant, which the CPB grants yearly based on relevant criteria.
- Member States can finance local holders of broadcasting licenses directly (the university TV stations or the local-community TV stations) or indirectly (in the case of State agencies that manage individual stations). Local governments finance TV stations run by the State schools. Regardless of the type of the licensee, the licensee must follow all local or national procedures (control) to expect financial support in the future.

20 One broadcasting license can be used by one or more TV stations.

- The funding share by the viewers collecting contributions to pay for the budget of local TV stations is steady growing. There are different ways of collecting contributions. The CPB even has a department that assists TV stations in collecting contributions from the public (such as by counselling, auctions, special events, TV programme that encourage contributing). Collecting contributions encourages donations by individuals, groups and different business systems.
- A method for funding public TVs (by redemption of debt) by various foundations, corporations, or business systems is becoming an important part of revenue in annual budgets. TV stations seek financial resources from large corporations for developing and producing specific programmes. The goal of a TV station and its sponsor is making certain contents for distribution to various TV stations through the CPB. Sponsors gain visibility and increase reputation in this way. However, due to their non-commercial nature, public TVs are limited in what and how much they can mention of the sponsors in their programmes. Sponsorship of programmes must not be recognizable as a commercial activity, but only as a purchase or facilitation of the production of certain programmes.
- Public TV stations in the multi-media market have to seek other funding opportunities and to provide additional services besides "traditional" contents. One of the options is a profit-making commercial production, carried out together with an additional corporation's organizational units. Additional activities comprise publications, rentals of rooms and equipment, and the use of additional up-to-date media platforms.

To fight the competition, the PBS associating various non-commercial TV stations in the United States had to seek additional funding resources by applying and converging new technologies. About half of the funds for CPS come from private sources (McKinsley, 2013).

Management strategies of various public TV stations try to fulfil two objectives – to pursue its mission and increase the chances of getting additional income. Management strategies, especially the programme strategies, vary from those used in the European public TV stations by the fact that the PBS, as an umbrella organization, "cares" for its members. TV stations get on average 64 percent of programme contents from the PBS. Regional associations produce programme contents for their members. The remaining programme contents come from other sources, depending on the type of the broadcasting licence, because universities, schools, and agencies produce programmes for their TV stations.

Editorial policies for classifying contents in programming schemes vary among TV stations according to the type of license and acquired programmes.

Their fundamental paradigm is not achieving the largest audience shares across the entire programming scheme, but meeting interests of varied minorities in different time spaces.

The ratings of US public TV stations and commercial stations are not comparable because these two categories are entirely different and also have different missions. However, reaching target groups is an important orientation also by managements of non-commercial stations at the local level. Governance in public TV stations has to track performance and efficiency criteria as in other commercial organizations.

European dual broadcasting system

European society treats traditional broadcasting service as an important social activity, founded with the purpose »to inform, teach, and entertain, and to provide a diverse (balanced) programme and 'universality ' in geographical terms.« (Dyson and Humpreys, 1988: 5). Both in the United States and Europe, television "inherited" the institutional status of radio as it was established between 1920 and 1935.

Broadcasting tightly relates to the facilitation of national identity and values. "Hence broadcasting is to be treated as a 'public good' that serves no one single vested interest, neither that of the government of the day nor that of a particular interest." (Dyson and Humpreys, 1988 : 11).

The traditional »dual system of the broadcasting policy« in Europe advocates the existence of one non-private and at least one private TV station in society. A non-private station is treated as a public broadcasting service. That means that it services the public interest and offers what the public needs at the same time. Such a "paternalistic" approach attributes a unique place to the non-private broadcasting service in society. Television often occupies a privileged position in society, which gives it a place of the keeper of "good taste" and "high" culture.

Dyson alleges (1988: 84) that the paternalistic concept of media policy originates from the period of the feudal and aristocratic Europe. This impact seems like turning back to the aristocratic way of perceiving and expressing an education and elite culture. Television as a mass medium has traditionally been an "ambassador of cultural values". Its behaviour is similar to that in the 19th century, when it was necessary to continuously represent and defend the ideal of "general culture" and the rule of language. The paternalistic concept also features in the Enlightenment idea of the public, which naively assumes that the masses would adopt the culture and political values of the elites. The same paternalistic concept strengthened in Europe after 1945 and dominated in the 1960s.

For the adoption of the dual system, particularly in order to preserve the public (state) television in Europe, we can find at least two sorts of arguments, the cultural and the political. Political arguments advocate the existence of public television, because the private media market is too unpredictable and too loose and permits monopolies. »To keep free elections and freedom of information necessary for election, it is vital to have the State television that is financed by the citizens and accountable to them by law. Such a TV should be one of the nation's institutions to feed the population with information, and only after this mission is achieved, private rivals could appear." (Haraszti, 1994).

There exist various types of broadcasting. First, there is the TV that is obliged by law to provide political information, and to be objective and impartial. Secondly, there are private TV channels that are not obliged by law to have a particular type of programme.

In the context of the public media remit, it is important to draw attention to the State broadcasters that were, until the late 1980's, central institutions in certain parts of Europe and the Soviet Union, in fact everywhere the public TVs did not broadcast. State broadcasting, often characterized as the third European broadcasting model is a precursor of public broadcasting, which emerged in the transition period of socio-political systems.

However, the most frequent argument for the existence of public television in Europe is cultural aspiration. Contrary to the US where there is no need to cultivate different cultures and languages, European countries are nation states in which national cultures and languages are to be protected.

The history of television in Europe stems from the idea of the public service. There exists no single theory or commonly accepted view about the obligations of public television. There are many versions of public television, depending on national priorities and traditions. A wide range of different organizational structures and national programmes that were in force until about 1980's were based on a common belief that all programmes had to fulfil the public interest. It was often implicitly assumed that diversity and quality applied to all programmes, including those for minorities.

In the early period, radio and later television were considered as the "public good", which should be available to all for the same price. Such a principle of universality also applies to water and electricity. Such an assumption is entirely different from that in the US, where the broadcasting was a commercial activity and was left to the free market rationale from its beginning. Most European countries treat radio and television programmes as the public good. Such a public good should however, be produced and broadcast by state-controlled mechanisms in special institutions and should not be left to a free-market rationale.

There exist various reasons for such a digression from the usual model of capitalist production that applies to other media, for example to print (Wieten et al., 2000). Restrictions on the sky posed the first obstacle, as there was less frequency spectrum than terrestrial space available. Therefore, someone had to define criteria and select users of the frequency spectrum. The scarcity of sources made it necessary to find a fair mechanism of selection, which was entrusted to the State as a representative and a guarantor of common interest. The public good and public service have reached convergence in broadcasting (Corcoran, 1996). The shocking experience of World War II, when Goebbels, the Minister of Propaganda in Nazi Germany, used the radio for the indoctrination of people, caused post-war television to opt for the intervention of the State. Hence, the public broadcasting system became extremely politicized because of State's intervention, and also the privileges and threats that the Government saw in this powerful medium.

Concerns relating to the limits of the sky were also present in other parts of the world, including the United States. Therefore, the Federal Communications Commission and a light-touch regulation were introduced in the US too. An analysis of the American (commercial) television model reveals an essential difference in the relationship between the State and capital in proportion to their powers.

The liaison between politics and broadcasting has not been the same in all European countries. Countries such as Great Britain, Ireland and Sweden had a more autonomous system (Wieten et al., 2000), which allowed the setting of mechanisms for withdrawing political groups from the broadcasting decision-making. Besides that, the political culture of these environments was also crucial. In Germany, Denmark, Belgium and the Netherlands, the ruling structures recruited representatives of key political and other social groups in broadcasting organizations. In Greece, Spain, Italy and France, national authorities had the power to intervene in the broadcasters' decisions. In the socialist countries of Central and Eastern Europe, broadcasting organizations had a legitimate position as State media and acted according to instructions of political leaders.

Despite political diversity, there are some outstanding similarities among European TV broadcasters, especially among the selected non-commercial, public and publicly funded institutions. The difficulty of defining the public service is explored in previous chapters. However, there exist a few common points.

In 1994, in Prague, at the European Ministerial Conference on mass media, the Council of Europe adopted a resolution that defined the characteristics of public television as a public service (Bašić-Hrvatin, 2002). Due to potential threats to its survival, attention was drawn to social and cultural objectives that legitimise the existence of rigid structures:

- Public service creates a common point of reference for the entire public, and thus for social cohesion and integration.
- It creates a forum for public debate.
- It reports on unbiased and independent news, information and provides commentaries;
- It develops pluralist, inventive and diverse programmes.
- It serves interests of the general public and enables the representation of all minority groups at the same time.
- It reflects the philosophical and religious beliefs of society as a whole;
- It contributes to a greater respect for and dissemination of the diversity of national and European cultural heritage.
- It supports audiovisual production, in particular movies and dramas, and other creative outputs.
- It offers programme services that commercial stations do not provide (Council of Europe, 1994).

These points of departure are primarily the norms, which national public TV broadcasters should meet. However, they operate within different national legal frameworks, subject to different standards and traditions, so their missions often hardly converge on the European tendencies. The resolution's definition can be understood as a set of cultural values that oppose the dominance of commercialization characterizing the American broadcasting model. Despite that, also in Europe, public TV stations are becoming just one of many players in the last decade.

Media systems have changed in all European countries. Today's Western Europe features a dual picture compared to the situation in 1980 characterized by public monopoly (with mostly mixed funding by subscriptions and advertising).

There exist different typologies of TV systems relevant to the sources of income (Siune and Hulten, 1998: 27). There are also some other key typologies based on purpose and institutional status. Programming directions defined by statutes and laws, and their institutional status, determine the purpose of TV institutions. In this respect, they are subject to monitoring and fulfilment of particular commitments. Besides, there also exist mixed types of broadcasters featuring the financial and the other two criteria. (Public TV, despite its mission and institutional status, can also earn income from advertising. On the other hand, commercial broadcasters can acquire a commitment to provide non-commercial contents or can even be partly public/State funded).

The relationship between the EU policy and public broadcasting service can be summarized as a historical dilemma providing no explicit answer. Moreover, there is still no guarantee that the active European anti-monopoly policy and the aspirations for the survival of public broadcasting service will be balanced.

Commercial broadcasters

The European media environment was marked by significant changes in the last decade. Technological developments in the cable and satellite broadcasting, as well as changes in the political climate, have opened up possibilities for expanding TV programmes. Gradually, commercial channels, local, national and international, have become dominant players in the media market. By the early 1980s, the public TV system dominated in 17 Western European countries. In 1980, only four commercial channels in three Member States (Luxembourg, Finland, and Great Britain) operated beside 40 public TV channels. This proportion changed at the end of the 20th century. Cable and satellite broadcasting, as well as the liberalized market, have paved the way for private companies in most West European countries and created a different TV system.

Reviews of the national terrestrial, cable and satellite broadcasting show that nearly 60 public and more than 70 private channels reach over 50 percent of households and aspire to the "national population", that means as many viewers as possible in the country. In addition, what is more, there are hundreds of private, mostly cable and satellite specialized channels that reach smaller shares of the population (music, sports, news) or just a regional audience.

The wire-cable penetration and sales of satellite dishes show the levels of economic development of individual countries, which also relates to the more or less restrictive national regulatory policies. In the past ten years, the number of paid channels has substantially increased. An explosion of channels and viewing options resulted commonly in an exceptionally significant drop in ratings of traditional national public TVs.

Structures of private TV channels vary from country to country since their institutional status and functioning depend on their national economic and political environments. They can be part of large international corporations or separate corporations with the controlling national ownership, and licensed for a national frequency or more regional frequencies. A few features divide public and private TV systems already at the points of departure. They are funding, accountability, and the mission expressed by the programming. In reality, the dichotomy between public and private derives from the conflict between public goals and private ambitions, between political beliefs and economic reality. It also comes from the tension between the free-market rationale and the State's interference, between the liberal and the interventionist perspective, as well as between the public good and competition.

The success of new commercial TV stations from the mid-1980s brought a drop in advertising revenues in public TV stations. The reductions in advertising revenue have caused the public service serious financial problems. Therefore, it started actively seeking other sources of income. The success of the first commercial stations also encouraged the arrival of a number of new commercial media players (cable and satellite providers). Erosion of the advertising market in the Digital Era will undoubtedly impose additional burdens on the survival of different channels (public and private).

The search for new possibilities of survival is the reason why commercial TV broadcasters have started offering new services. The public will not spend more time than today watching traditional TV programmes. The plentiful supply of programmes will encourage viewers to demand a higher value for the time devoted to programmes. The principles governing paid and unpaid programmes are similar. With paid programmes, viewers require adequate value for their money, while with unpaid programmes they require adequate value for the time spent.

Commercial broadcasters often claim that it is they, who produce the real public television, as they know and offer what the public wants. Commercial broadcasters sell their products with the aim of making a profit, and have to report only to their owners. They estimate their performance according to the audience share they reach, the costs, revenues and annual profits. Therefore, the responsibility of the commercial broadcasting relates only to attracting the audience and providing the revenue. Responsibility of public broadcasting is complex. Its guiding idea is that the subscription for the public good requires the meeting of the public requirements and expectations. A look at conditions in European countries reveals in the first place political responsibility and to a lesser extent responsibility to the audience. Political responsibility is exercised through political institutions, such as ministries, Parliament or political groups, to which broadcasting services are accountable (Mitchell and Blumler, 1994). Responsibility to viewers so far has not been a priority in the policy of most public-service broadcasters in Europe, since their market shares or ratings did not play a decisive role in their programming policies.

Each TV organization, private or public, follows its mission. Commercial broadcasters are often targets of criticism, saying that their mission is only to provide a programme that people want. In pursuing particular viewing shares, programming strategies of commercial broadcasters follow the policy of how to "sell" their viewers to advertisers in the best possible way. Their policy concentrates on two demographic categories: the size and structure of the audience the advertisers are interested in, related to the customers' potential and their impact in society. Here, policy often diverges, since populist programmes, such as sport and entertainment, usually gain significant advertising shares. On the other hand, the programmes attracting the "quality" public (opinion makers and viewers with higher purchasing power) are specially designed for demanding viewers (news, current, cultural, art programmes). Thus, commercial strategies must ensure the maximum possible size of the audience (provide entertainment contents) and quality programmes at the same time.

Despite the fact that it is difficult to compare the performance of TV stations due to different national regulatory frameworks, the main difference between the two models is in the proportion of programmes. Commercial stations broadcast larger shares of entertainment contents, while informative and artistic programmes prevail on public broadcasts. In the last decade, public-service broadcasters provide more entertainment contents, thereby responding to commercial rivals. A common feature of commercial stations is also that most of their drama broadcasts are of US origin.

The European media environment was marked by significant changes in the last decade. A monopoly situation, in which public TV broadcasters mostly received income from both sources (subscription and advertising), has evolved towards today's situation in which they have to share revenue with the growing number of commercial TV players. Significant changes in commercial and public organizations adapting to new circumstances have caused a blurring of differences between the private profit-driven TVs and the public-funded TVs that follow their cultural and educational mission. Examples of the British Channel 4, the Swedish TV 4, and the Finnish MTV 3 suggest a third option for commercial stations. Their strategy differs from both the "pure" non-commercial public TV broadcasters and the "pure" profit-oriented commercial stations by its combining of strict criteria of fulfilling the public mission and the profit-oriented rationale.

Public-service broadcasters

Public television is at the heart of political debate in many European countries and political decisions at the European level, as it is the core player in media environments of all European countries. It closely relates to the countries' media policies from the start, when a monopoly TV system with a single operating TV broadcaster was put into place. Being integrated in the socio-political system, the TV system is subject to all social changes. The development of public TVs was influenced by many environmental impacts. The most important in the last decade are the following:

- *Implementing new technologies:* digital television and in particular the Internet have a significant impact on traditional media. Despite fundamental differences between Member States in the development and use of new technologies, the new technologies will undoubtedly play a vital role in dissemination of contents. Providing contents via other channels (platforms) raises the demand for a new definition of traditional television.
- *Political and economic factors* have played an important role. From the early 1980s, liberalization was the primary focus of media policies. *Globalization* of the media industry and the *convergence* of different media and telecommunications have resulted in the integration of markets and corporations. Liberal legislation and integration of markets and corporations create different relationships among commercial and public competitors in the media market.
- *Cultural factors* are often underestimated compared to the technological, political and economic. Individualized lifestyles in European cultures have strongly impacted individuals' choice of media contents and caused *segmentation* of the audience. The public needs require public TVs to consider how to produce adequate programming in a changed environment.

While these issues are relevant both to the public and to the private sector, the public sector additionally has to face many dilemmas arising from the *legislative framework* and their *organizational structure.*

- Public television tries to respond to the *competitive* environment. Legislation defines the limits of adjustment to the competitive environment.
- The financial sources of public TVs vary, but their problems are common, namely the growing costs and uncertainty about future revenues.
- There are many ways how a public TV could operate more efficiently and adapt to the competitive environment. However, there exists no ideal model.

Despite the fact that public TVs are key players in the European media market, there is no commonly accepted model or a definition of the public TV broadcasting service.

Funding

The public TV model dominated in Europe until the mid-1980s, with the exception of Luxembourg's CTL (RTL), which had a private TV since its foundation in 1929. In most countries, public-service broadcasters used to hold a monopoly status, being primarily financed by subscriptions. Such revenues are mainly collected by official bodies or the TV corporations themselves. In most countries, however, Parliament fixes the amount that belongs to the public TV (Wieten et al., 2000).

The reduction in non-commercial funding has caused public-service broadcasters to become more and more dependent on advertising revenue, which is, however, not easily achievable due to new commercial players in the market. That is why most of today's public TV stations in Europe have to cope with organizational and financial issues. In Europe, there exist four sources of funding: licence fee or subscription, Government grants, advertising, and other sources[21]. However, there exists no established, so-called optimal model of public TV funding. The European public-service broadcasters are undoubtedly under intense pressure because of unpredictable funding in the future. The survey, produced by McKinsey Corporation (1999: 25–32) and commissioned by the BBC, describes models of the public TV funding in the future. The survey exposes advertising as a very unstable means of funding, since it depends on the economic cycles in the market and is vulnerable to a variety of pressures by competition. Government grants are also an unstable source, since their level depends on current Government policies. With such funding, public-service broadcasters are also subject to general economic conditions and political pressures. A licence fee is a more stable and predictable source of funding than the other two ways, but it does not require the service provider to observe the audience's wishes (Bašić Hrvatin, 2002: 49).

A licence fee is the most secure and reliable source of TV funding. It enables particular contents to be safeguarded from abolition due to market conditions. However, it causes less discipline in performance, demanding no permanent checking of their market efficiency. Business incomes (from advertising for example) on the other hand are a much more unreliable source of funding since they "force" the broadcasters towards a market-driven operation.

Accountability

The accountability of public TV stations, particularly those receiving income from the budget or fees, is subject to the activity and understanding of the ruling group. That means that public TV stations in many countries are supposed to be still quite politicized.

The objectives of the public broadcasting service adopted at the Ministerial Conference in Prague (1994) set points of departure for European public TVs. They should follow a mission comprising at least three elements: a cultural and pedagogical logic, their position in civil society and their contribution to social

21 Typical other sources are sales of various commercial products, services or programmes.

cohesion (Wieten et al., 2000: 16). The cultural and pedagogical logic is part of the Enlightenment ideal of a country's prosperity. TV programmes must serve the public interest, and not necessarily, what the public would want. Their mission is to educate, inform and enrich the public with culture. TV can be part of the fun too, however only when the contents reach a high-quality level. Such a "paternalistic" perspective attributes a unique place in society to the European television.

The function of TV in democratic society is to work for democracy and allow citizens to participate in societal democratic processes. Public television has to provide programmes for everyone, special programmes for minorities, programmes that strengthen national and cultural heritage, and programmes that take account of minority cultural interests and are welcome to society as a whole.

Elements of the public television mission are embedded in the operation and programming of various TV stations. Programming and production outputs of European public TV broadcasters differentiate substantially, but there are a few common tendencies too. Commercial TV stations, in comparison with the public TVs, invest fewer budgets in the original production and more in the purchase of foreign programmes.

Public TV stations, on the other hand, largely broadcast news and more art, drama, religious and children's contents than commercial rivals do. Such a generalization, however, cannot give a clear picture, while a glance through the offering of individual public TVs shows different programming according to national legislations, budgeting and production resources; how they respond to the competition, and how they reflect the tradition and political culture of their environments. Their common characteristic is news, current affairs and entertainment programmes, and films that occupy the largest share of the offer.

The more or less rigid programming schemes of public TV broadcasters reflect their viewing shares too. The decline started in the mid-1990's because of new commercial rivals. The viewing results demonstrate the varied positions of public TV broadcasters, depending on social factors of their national environments. In some markets for example, the public TVs hold such a firm position due to their tradition and quality that even the most aggressive commercial rivals achieve lower ratings.

All public TVs are firmly embedded in their national environments, which affect their development. Therefore, it is difficult to talk about a general model of development. Despite that, it is possible to highlight a few common characteristics of the dynamic European media environment that indicate a tendency towards transformation of public television.

Trends in the dual broadcasting system

A media environment with both public and commercial players introduces mechanisms that do not differentiate between public and commercial broadcasters. First, viewers choose the contents that meet their interests from the whole »television landscape«, and not from a particular broadcaster, no matter whether it be commercial or public.[22] Secondly, the emergence of commercial TV players also affects the public TV programming, pushing less attractive contents to less friendly viewing hours, and thus introducing new benchmarks that prevail in society. Competition among programme contents has moved to the scheduling of individual channels too.

European public TV broadcasters seek their opportunities in a media remit that was significantly affected by commercial actors in the last decade. Their operation must be competitive and complementary in relation to private TV stations. According to Blumler (Blumler, 1992: 206), policies of public TVs must reflect a balanced relationship between competitiveness and complementarity. Competitiveness refers to the products that enterprises offer and users accept. Hence, TV programmes are also considered as competitive. One of the criteria must additionally be a viewing share, since a TV broadcaster cannot act as a social institution if it does not meet interests of the majority. Important criteria for competitiveness undoubtedly remain the quality, innovation, professionalism, standards and compliance with various social interests (Blumler, 1992). A complementary function derives from the fact that public TVs facilitate the values that private TV's do not support because they do not invest much in innovative programmes. Public-service broadcasters must adapt to the new market conditions featuring private corporations, commercialization, and internationalization. Such a competitive environment forces also public TV stations to track the market-driven rationale. On the other hand, it is also obvious that the new system takes care of an individual and his/her wishes, which were overshadowed by other politically relevant decisions in the previous system.

McQuail (2001) explains that the public television has lost its role as a model and as a reference to the other systems. He emphasizes that it is difficult to find support for the old TV system that was characterized by monopoly, public funding, programmes for the elite, closed access and slow technological development. Such a system required changes in many areas in the 1990s.

---

22 *Viewing by appointment* is an approach used by TV corporations in designing their programming. They record the selection of programmes (viewing) based on adequate contents and not affiliation to a particular institution (Hujanene, 2002).

Public TV stations and their competitors operate in a society that has to cope with the following technological, political, economic and socio-cultural changes (Žilič Fišer, 2007).

1. *Technological changes:*
   - digitization
   - convergence of the computer technology, telecommunications and TV (media) sector

2. *Political and economic changes*:
   - liberalization
   - globalization
   - economic convergence (easier access to new markets and encouragement of synergies for value-added services and products)
   - integration of markets and companies, which results in concentration and outsourced operations

3. *Socio-cultural changes:*
   - individualization of lifestyles and segmentation of society,
   - effects on expansion and consumption (use) of the TV,
   - changes in scheduling

Various societal changes have affected media players and significantly marked the future development of public TVs. Runar Woldt (1998): 28) emphasizes three key dilemmas that are common to all European public broadcasters: competitiveness, financing and restructuring.

1. *Competitiveness:*
   - TV stations already compete for the audience, which is measured by viewing shares and rarely by qualitative indicators.
   - TV stations compete for advertising income.
   - TVs compete for resources, especially for programmes and creative individuals.

2. *Funding:*
   - Licence fee (a key topic of debate in most European countries, referring to its legitimacy and amount)
   - advertising revenue
   - sponsorship
   - direct income from the state budget
   - commercial activities

3. *Restructuring:*

- Restructuring of the whole sector meaning a change of TV programmes within the national TV system and the redefinition of the social mission and commitments of all TV programmes;
- Internal restructuring, meaning a change of management methods and strategies aimed at greater economic efficiency and competitiveness;
- Localizing and globalizing, meaning to solve a dilemma whether local, regional and national public broadcasters should observe the particular needs of these publics, although they must compete with dominating private transnational corporations in the same market;
- Defining modes of collaboration between the public and private sector.

These are the common points of departures for the change of all public TV broadcasters in Europe. However, the circumstances they have to operate in and respond to are different. Each public TV broadcaster works in a national environment, which features the following particularities:

- legislative framework (media legislations in Europe vary greatly between the Member States),
- political climate,
- economic conditions,
- infrastructure and
- language and culture

The study of common features and trends of public broadcasters in Europe could be started only after these peculiarities have been considered.

The public TV stations that succeeded in keeping their unique programme policy and observing the viewing criterion were the most successful. Better results also achieve those organizations that observe technological change and introduce new technologies in their operations. Introducing technological developments and offering digital channels provide the traditional public TV with additional services and results in more effective management strategies. The trends of advertising revenues in the media industry forecast a significant increase in the TV industry, since the other segments of traditional media are losing audience share to the benefit of TV advertising. The global economic crisis in 2008 and 2009 caused a drastic cut in advertising shares at all levels. However, the recovery recorded in individual environments in 2013 forecasts a rapid rise (McKinsey & Company, 2013). Central and Eastern Europe and Latin America plan a significant growth in income in 2015 and 2016.

TV system in the UK

Many of the debates about media systems focus on the British TV system. »The British have the best TV in the world.« (Goodwin, 1998 : 12) Television undoubtedly became a universal medium in Britain earlier than in other European countries. The model of the BBC organization served in the past as the main alternative to the commercial television model in the United States, and as a model of public television, which other European countries wanted to emulate.

Media in 20th century Britain underwent significant and slow change. That was a continuous evolution with political consensus (Tunstall, 1997). That large but gradual change, as well as the British traditionalism, completely differed from developments in other West European countries in the same century. Another significant characteristic besides gradation is a compromise between the commercial and the public service TV models.

Social change strongly marked the operation of television in the UK since its inception in 1936. With the advent of Mrs. Margaret Thatcher to power in 1979, capitalism followed the policy of privatization and deregulation stemming from the belief that the market should have free rein in all areas. Health care began to operate according to the free-market rationale, as well as the educational system, and finally the public television service got competitors in the national market. The rule of Margaret Thatcher marked British society and its ideology (Hood and Tabary-Peterssen, 1997: 28). The free-market policy in the media industry was a response to the needs and pressures of mainstream economic and political forces demanding UK competitiveness in the national and international markets.

The BBC started broadcasting from Alexandra Palace in November 1936, and that represented the start of public television in general. The Television Act of 1954 launched the *Independent Television Authority* (ITA).[23] ITV began broadcasting in September 1955 as the first commercial television.

The history of television in the UK can be divided into four periods:

1. BBC monopoly (1936–1955),
2. duopoly of ITV and the BBC (1955–1982),
3. deregulation and uncertainty (1982 to about 2000),
4. digital era (2000 and onwards)

The first period consists of the monopoly of BBC broadcasting. The second begins with the foundation of ITV commercial television in 1955. The duopoly

---

23 ITA renamed to Independent Broadcasting Authority (IBA) in July 1972 when took control over the operation of the broadcasting sector.

lasted until 1982 and provided equal shares of viewers for both the commercial and the public systems, without risking the survival of either. Their duopoly survived the arrival of the BBC 2 in 1964, but the launching of Channel 4 in 1982 endangered it. The three institutions, public, commercial and the public-commercial started a fierce battle for audiences during the third period of deregulation and uncertainty. Channel 5, launched in 1997, fragmented the public even more. The digital era started in 2000 with the search for solutions and adequate responses to technological and economic changes in the UK. Today, all of the terrestrial TVs have to cope with aggressive TV satellite and cable channels.

In the British media environment, commercial broadcasters must also observe provisions regarding programme contents, funding and fulfilment of social interest. The broadcasting regulatory framework in the UK tends to provide a broad scope of public television services, which in turn imposes a particular social mission on commercial broadcasters too. That means that the operation of the public (BBC) and the commercial broadcasters (ITV, Channel 5) actually overlaps, while the Channel Four Television Corporation most successfully succeeds in reconciling tensions between the free market rationale and the particular commitments of the public TV service.

Today, a host of TV channels fulfils various social missions; therefore, the public TV service is not simply a set of contents, but a competitive system providing for the creation of different programmes. A particular social mission imposed on broadcasters (commercial and public) at varying degrees needs support today more than ever. In the digitized media environment, television has ceased to be a "unique good".

BBC as an incumbent public service broadcaster

In 1922, the British Broadcasting Company was founded as a private monopoly corporation, and four years later it was transformed into a public company – the British Broadcasting Corporation (BBC).

The Government put in place the first director general, John Reith, who, with his vision and strategy, marked the ideology of public television as a public service. Television meant to him a special cultural and public mission, and a clear responsibility of the educated and cultural elite to use television for the enlightenment of the whole society. His belief was to give the public not what it wanted, but what it should have since only few knew, what they wanted and even fewer what they needed (Reith, 1924: 34). The Reithian vision, indeed, included a definition of democracy, but excluded the idea of choice. The Reithian vision advocates that only a monopoly run by professionals can ensure high-quality standards.

Due to the prevailing Reithian ideology and the institutional nature of the sole public-service corporation, television was considered as a public service and the public good too. After the end of the BBC monopoly, however, the link between television and the ideology of the exclusive public service became more problematic, because broadcasting ceased to be tied to a single institution.

The BBC is a public corporation and a non-profit organization funded by the citizens' income, as everyone owning a radio or a TV receiver is obliged to pay the television licence fee.

The BBC public service corporation used to be controlled by 12 Governors, appointed by The Queen on the advice of ministers. Governors would appoint the Director-General and other members of the executive board; set key objectives, strategies and policies, and supervise the Corporation. Based on the Royal Charter of 2006, the BBC is governed by the BBC Trust and managed by the Executive Committee. The BBC Trust is a safeguard of the public interest and the licence fee. The BBC was constituted by Royal Charter[24], which was supplemented by a Framework Agreement setting out in detail editorial independence and programme obligations. The BBC's programme obligations are quite loose compared to the obligations of other (commercial) players, and do not contain detailed provisions on hours and quota of programmes.

Commercial television

The outstanding feature of the British television, compared to other European TVs, is its early abolition of a monopoly status and launch of a dual TV system with commercial television. The BBC enjoyed its monopoly position until 1955, when the first commercial television, ITV, came on air based on the Television Act of 1954. The reason for its creation was the aspiration towards a free-market operation and criticism of the non-profit public service BBC (Goodwin, 1999; Block, 2001; Hood and Tabary-Peterssen, 1997).

Fifteen regional companies (holding regional broadcasting licenses) joined in the national network and made up a joint programming scheme that was funded by advertising revenues. Despite the private ownership and profit-driven strategy, ITV has to observe certain directives of public television service stipulated

24 The current Royal Charter is accessible at www.bbc.co.uk http://downloads.bbc.co.uk/bbctrust/assets/files/pdf/about/how_we_govern/charter.pdf. The current Royal Charter was adopted in 2006 and runs until 2016.

by the *Independent Broadcasting Authority* (IBA), and its successor, the *Independent Television Commission* (ITC).[25]

The ITC used to hold a broad and powerful range of authority, granting frequency licences, deciding on programme obligations, and monitoring the commercial sector. One of the challenges was also the stability of the duopoly system, which was achieved by financial regulation. The BBC is funded solely from television licence fees, while ITV companies had a monopoly in the advertising market. Such a conscious avoidance of direct competition in the advertising market provided both corporations with economic security, and led to a programming policy that aimed not only at maximizing the audience but also at fulfilling the public interest (responsibilities of public television service).

The arrival of ITV was a tremendous challenge for the BBC, despite the fact that they did not compete for the audience share in the advertising market. They significantly differed in contents, especially in the entertainment programmes and news. ITV News soon reached a larger viewing share, and gradually both of the TV broadcasters evenly shared the audience. Despite the private ownership and profit-driven strategy, ITV's programmes considerably differ from commercial TVs in other European countries with respect to their quality and quantity; hence, the ITV network transmits the largest share of non-commercial contents (Davis, 1991: 51).

ITV's obligations stem from the frequency licence granted. Implementation of its provisions and the extensive additional programme and corporate requirements, however, were supervised by the ITC, and now by the Ofcom. The implementation of these provisions and observance of market principles were quite easy until the arrival of new competitors - Channel 4 (public-commercial television) and Channel 5 (commercial television).

Hybrid broadcasting model

In the 1970s, the British Government announced the launching of another TV channel and started a debate about the destiny, operating conditions and the purpose of

25 IBA was succeeded by ITC pursuant to the Broadcasting Act of 1990. ITC used to grant frequency licenses to commercial TV publishers and monitored their operation. From December 2003, it ended its duties together with four other regulatory bodies. All regulatory powers were transferred to Ofcom, a UK communications regulator, in accordance with the new media legislation. The research took place during the period of previous regulatory bodies; therefore, it refers to the former regulators, mainly to ITC.

the fourth channel. The Report[26] stating conditions and opportunities of the new channel revealed high tensions between the broadcasting executive board and the Government. The powerful BBC, which justified all its operations by the particular mission it had been given, also needed a counter-balance. (Goodwin, 1998). At the same time, there was no intention to reinforce the commercial sector, which was the powerful domain of ITV. What was needed was a creative institution that could tap into all the creative potential that could not find space on the BBC or ITV.

Channel 4, fulfilling a particular social mission as a public broadcasting service and at the same time operating as a commercial broadcaster, proves to be an excellent model to study the management and principles of television functioning. Channel 4 is a corporation founded by the state with a particular social mission. At the same time, its performance exclusively depends on its economic efficiency, since advertising income is its sole source funding. It is treated as a commercial, public-service broadcasting service.

Historical justification for the creation of Channel 4

An overview of the media circumstances can reveal the reasons for the launch of a new programme. In the 1960s, the Conservative government established a Committee on Broadcasting[27], which examined conditions after commercial TVs entered the market and decided who should allocate and run a third television programme. In its report of 1962, it recommended that the following television programme be awarded to the BBC.

In 1971, a coalition of people assembled to consider the future of the British broadcasting. A long debate and examination of the media situation revealed the need for another television programme to counterbalance transmissions of the public-service BBC and commercial ITV. They also led to common aspirations for the fourth channel, which were published by the memorandum Opportunities for the fourth channel (Blanchard and Morley, 1982: 45).

Public debates and committee decisions at that time could be summarized in the following aspirations for the fourth channel (Lambert, 1982: 5–73):

1. The fourth channel should be the "fourth power«, encouraging innovation and giving a chance to alternative sources.
2. It should be independent of the existing ITV companies and from the Independent Broadcasting Authority (IBA).

---

26 The Annan Report on the opportunities of Channel 4 (Goodwin, 1999, Hood and Tabary-Peterssen, 1997).
27 Led by Sir Harry Pilkington.

3. It should have a flexible structure providing enough financial resources and a strong production base.
4. Its programming scheme should be complementary to give the viewers an alternative to the ITV and the BBC programmes.
5. It should provide a full range of programmes that take account of particular interests and at the same time not ignore common interests and popular programmes.

In 1977, the Open Broadcasting Authority (OBA) was founded, based on the report by Lord Annan's Committee; its primary task was to decide on the allocation of the fourth channel. After many years of debate and planning, The Queen in Her speech of May 1979 announced that legislation should pave the way for the operation of the fourth broadcasting service, which should be subject to strict control. The Broadcasting Act published in 1980 comprised all the amendments to the Act of 1973.

Channel Four Television Corporation came into being in January 1981 under the leadership of Chief Executive Jeremy Isaacs. Channel 4 at its creation featured the following characteristics and goals:

- the viewing share planned to 10–15 percent;
- target audience different from other television programmes; programmes designed primarily for youth, elderly people and ethnic groups;
- Channel 4 was created as a publisher not producing its own contents but promoting and transmitting British independent production (buying programmes from independent production companies);
- independent production should have the largest share of all TV contents transmitted by Channel 4.

The decision on the formation of the fourth channel is a reflection of the historical, political, cultural and economic situation in Great Britain in the late 1970s. The need to counterbalance the functioning of the commercial and the public service television, and give space to another commercial television station in the advertising market appeared during the late 1970s and early 1980s. The most important driving force for the creation of the fourth channel was the lobby group of British independent production companies pushing for a larger share in the British TV programming schemes. BBC's collaboration with external production houses was rather poor as it increased own production base from year to year. ITV also worked with just a few major external production houses because it sourced its own production from regional ITV companies.

Channel 4 was meant to fill the gap in the British production industry. The broadening of the production base and the encouragement of creative production were politically justified reasons for launching a new television channel. There is no doubt that the economic, cultural and historical circumstances were relevant, but the most crucial was the political decision that laid stress on concern for the British people and various minorities in society. Political forces considered the creation of a new public television programme Channel 4 as one of the most important and appropriate political decisions in early 1980s (Goodwin, 1999; Isaacs, 1989; Harvey, 2000; Docherty and Morrison, 1988).

Historical funding formula

The IBA stipulated and supervised a special funding agreement that came in force in April 1986 and ran to 31 December 1992. Channel 4 was funded by the ITC, which collected subscription for the fourth channel from ITV companies. The agreed amount was a 17 percent (NAR)[28] share of all ITV companies, together with the Channel 4's advertising revenue.[29] As a result of such a funding arrangement, Channel 4 received 80 percent of all subscriptions to the fourth channel amounting to 17 percent NAR.

In January 1993, Channel 4 started selling its advertising airtime alone. Then, a particular funding formula was introduced according to which Channel 4 had to pay half of its advertising income to ITV should its income rise above the 14 percent threshold of NAR. The funding formula applied to the whole revenue of ITV, Channel 4, Channel 5 and S4C from advertising and sponsorship. The Broadcasting Act also stipulated that ITV should pay Channel 4 up to two percent of NAR if Channel 4's revenue reached less than 14 percent threshold of NAR in a calendar year. Its purpose was to balance the advertising market.

The Broadcasting Act determined proportions within the funding formula, which should change over the years. However, Channel 4 led a successful campaign to abolish the funding formula. The reason for its abolition was in the Channel 4's efficient operation that needed no subsidies from ITV. On the contrary, Channel 4 was obliged to pay surplus advertising income to ITV every year. In February 1999, Channel 4 made the last payment (£ 66 million) to ITV pursuant to the funding formula, which the Broadcasting Act of 1990 introduced.

---

28 NAR as *net advertising revenues*

29 Subscription to the fourth channel was used partly (20 percent) for the funding of the Welsh Fourth Channel Authority, S4C (the Scottish Channel 4) and the rest for Channel 4.

Channel 4 succeeded in convincing[30] the Government to abolish the funding formula and all the "funding valves" that prevented Channel 4 from operating autonomously in the market. The ITC renewed the operating license pursuant to new conditions published on 23 February 1998, and determined additional commitments requiring transmissions of more British-originated programmes. In addition, it granted a digital multiplex channel license.[31] Channel 4 got an additional obligation to invest the surplus advertising revenue (not needed to be paid to ITV anymore) in new technologies and new pay and interactive services. That resulted in the launching of the FilmFour in November 1999.

Legal obligations and monitoring of Channel 4

Channel 4 came on air in 1982 as a publisher under the Broadcasting Act of 1980, which imposed the obligation to:

- provide an appropriate proportion of contents that were not usually transmitted by ITV
- ensure a reasonable proportion of educational contents, and
- encourage innovation

In 1999, additional obligations were imposed:

- 60 percent of the airtime should be ordered, and at least 25 percent of the programmes should come from independent producers.
- Repeats should not exceed 40 percent of the programme transmitted.

Broadcasting licence for Channel 4

The decision on the allocation of the broadcasting licence comprises instructions for programme obligations, the school and educational programmes, the news, documentaries, religious and multicultural programmes and investments in film.[32] Channel 4 has to:

- have a distinctive, own identity,
- transmit various services including news, educational, religious and multicultural contents in primetime hours,
- give education a central position in its programming,
- be the mainstream player in the British film industry,

30 In fact, it was a yearlong lobbying campaign, in which various civil associations, professional and academic circles took part.

31 ITC granted the digital multiplex channel licence in 1997.

32 Key programme obligations of Channel 4 are listed in Enclosure 2.

- encourage a broad and diverse independent production industry and production outside London,
- Channel 4 shall observe specific provisions on originated production, purchasing of programmes, education and programmes for people with particular needs.

Monitoring of Channel 4 draws attention to its particular dual character as a public television service that is subject to strict programming criteria, and as a commercial television that is subject to commercial rationale.

Unique identity of Channel 4 in the British media market

- Channel 4 was founded by the State, and it operates as a public television.
- It competes in the advertising market for advertising share, and thus acts as a public commercial television.
- Channel 4 was constituted as a publisher of programme contents and not as a broadcasting company.
- It is the third largest commercial television corporation in Great Britain.
- Compared to ITV, Channel 4 has outstanding competitive advantages since a small group of directors manages it. It has much lower administrative costs, and in contrast with other commercial TVs, it attracts high-quality audience that is targeted by most advertisers.
- Compared to BBC, it has many advantages: a smaller and more efficient organizational structure and more attractive audience.
- Channel 4 worked as a technological and programme experiment in media environment in UK and all over the world.

Independent production companies

The essential reason for the survival and growth of independent production sector is its contractual relationship with the broadcasting industry. Separation between production and broadcasting contributes to the market competitiveness in both the US and the UK. In the UK, this separation took place by two steps:

- by founding Channel 4 in 1981, and
- by introducing a proportion of independent production in the BBC programming from October 1987

A new form of television industry went hand in hand with the idea of the industry's regeneration (Block 2001: 19). Small and medium-sized enterprises seemed to be the best tool to revitalize the British industry.

A production base attracting creative and innovative forces is an essential driver of TV's development. Independent production companies made a revolutionary leap in television production by the migration of creative forces from large production bases (BBC, ITV) to small independent production centres with rented crews and production equipment. The independent production sector managed to optimize the use of production resources and adapt more quickly to new technologies and development work models, which resulted in reduced production costs and increased yield. The independent production sector also contributed to cultural change by offering programmes that could not be found on the BBC or ITV. Many high-quality documentaries on ethnic and other peculiarities in society found their place in the TV programming. The needs of TV houses also changed, as the changed regulatory policy encouraged a closer collaboration between independent production companies and TV organizations.

Thus, a small number (300) of active production houses in Britain grew to more than 1,000 within a few years (Block, 2001: 24). After the great expansion, their number slowly began to stabilize. Rapid changes in the media market caused integration of production companies too, and the biggest actors got access to TV stations and their programme.

The existence of an independent production sector can also be justified on economic and cultural grounds as it reduces purchases of cheap American contents and encourages British-originated production. By imposing on TV a greater accountability for domestic production, the Government made this requirement easier by stimulating the growth of the independent production sector. The power of the independent production sector is in its rapid adaptability to change; the weakness, however, is in its specialization and focusing on market segments.

Such a particular cultural, political and economic environment in the UK apparently led to the formation of a dynamic television system, in which the public-commercial television also found space and could strengthen its position. Explanation of the circumstances surrounding the Channel Four Television Corporation allows a better understanding of its functioning, which the following chapters will explore.

The next chapter will display criteria proposed for the evaluation of a television organization that functions as a public service, and is subjected to the free market rationale because of massive technological, economic and socio-political change.

5. Evaluating the Performance of Media Organizations

This chapter deals with the reasons for taking account of economic criteria in evaluating the effectivity of management in public television. Economic indicators are essential in figuring out how a television organization integrates into a dynamic media environment; nevertheless, their role is often overlooked. Defining criteria for measuring the effects of various management practices is crucial to the understanding of a modern management process.

Studies using political criteria point to the fulfilment of public interest that society imposes on the public-service broadcaster as one of dominant social institutions. At the same time, market liberalism requires stricter performance criteria for the study of public service institutions. The growing liberalization pushes public-service broadcasters to earn their financial resources in the free market, and imposes on them the same management criteria as on commercial players. Adaptation to the market conditions is the most important indicator of success. Observing economic criteria is vitally important for the public broadcasting service, because it shows its responsibility to the public and society. It demonstrates itself in the ability of an organization to adapt to conditions of both the national and global market.

In assessing media management strategies, the following criteria are helpful: market share criteria to assess ratings, criteria of productivity to assess the effectiveness of financial and programme resources, financial criteria to monitor the revenue growth, and management criteria to assess technological potentials and accumulation of reserves. Management criteria used to assess performance output are helpful in analyzing the management process of an organization, and in assessing managerial approaches at different levels of a television organization. This kind of criteria will contribute to a detailed analysis of the management process of the Channel Four Television Corporation.

The unique nature of the broadcasting sector requires additional criteria for the study and evaluation of management and performance output of public broadcasting service fulfilling the mission of public good and simultaneously observing free market principles. All these criteria make it possible to analyze the broadcaster's management process and to show its strengths and weaknesses.

The European public broadcasting remit faced turbulent changes over the last decade for two main reasons: Public service broadcasters increased the number of TV programmes, and market liberalization caused expansion of commercial programmes at the global, national and local level. Besides, cable and satellite services became more accessible than in the 1980s. All these changes have contributed to a stronger competition for the audience and larger viewing shares. Public service broadcasters, which used to have almost monopoly position two decades ago, have equal status to other market players today. The following pages are devoted mainly to the *management of a broadcaster in changed market circumstances.* Most studies on the public service broadcasters often neglect the importance of the market and viewing shares concentrating only on assessing their role and significance.

When a television programme records a drop in market share in a stable market, it is high time to check its performance. Such a fall often indicates a lower quality service, less attractive programming or a loss of contact with the audience. These are the signals pointing to a television organization losing its position in the market and wider society. Some also forecast black scenarios if commercial broadcasting sector fails to deliver to users what they want, and if public broadcaster loses the public support because it fails to serve the public interest. A drop in ratings could be understood in the case of major changes caused by new market players. However, also in such a case, it is vital to reconsider the business and media strategies.

Comparing broadcasters' performance operating in different national markets is rather difficult, since they differ by the number of channels, population, traditions, and different societal, cultural, social, and political demands towards public broadcasting services. Nevertheless, this book sheds light on some common starting points that allow determination of criteria for the performance effectivity of public service broadcasters.

Public support for public television

In today's host of television channels with a variety of programmes, public television is just one among the players in the market. Its role is not self-evident, since its mission alone does not justify its existence and is not indispensable either. In today's audiovisual era, there are mixed views on the need and role of public service broadcasting. Who or what justifies its existence: social mission or public needs? Who defines public needs and in what way? Do public needs mean the same as a social mission of a public service broadcasting (PSB)? These dilemmas reflect society, which changes its requirements towards PSB and urges a redefinition of its role.

The public's attitude towards social developments and services is changing. Privatization of the telecommunications industry, banks, postal systems, transport services and systems of social welfare has a crucial impact on society's attitude towards institutions of special social importance.

Public television systems represent a rather small share of the audiovisual industry. Private media criticize PSM at various levels. They often attack the exclusive position of the public broadcasting service and urge its sharper regulation while requiring a light-touch control for private broadcasters.

These debates usually do not deny the need for public broadcasting service in society, but concentrate mainly on the performance effectivity of a PSB. The purpose of the study is to justify the need for *effective* performance by the public broadcasting service (PSB). Performance effectivity and execution of tasks assure:

- increasing credibility of public broadcasting
- preserving its legitimacy in society
- meeting clear criteria of performance assessment

PSBs in Europe obtain funding resources in different ways. However, their budgets mostly consist of non-commercial income. Subscription or government subventions impose on public institutions particular accountability. That means that their performance has to be needed and justified by society. If PSBs did not satisfy any needs and tastes of society, their operation would be purposeless, and illegitimate. The legitimacy of their operation is related to the presenting of certain societal interests too. If an institution serves the needs of the largest social group, there is a greater chance that its public funding would be accepted as justified.

In today's market-driven society with a host of private players tracking an economic rationale and the highest possible cost-efficiency, it is obvious to transmit such a rationale from the private to the public service. Mixing private and public managerial practices requires, in addition, the setting of more appropriate criteria for performance assessment of a large number of social services, from educational to health-care institutions.

New managerial practices bring essential changes in PSBs in respect of their tradition and organizational culture. According to Hujanen, organizational change relates to a new identity of television as a cultural institution, in contrast with former perceptions of its state bureaucratic form (Hujanen, 2002: 87). The growing competition among programmes is due to the core process of transformation of public broadcasting from a national to a cultural character. The European broadcasting industry is a result of technological and economic change in the global market, and of regulatory and deregulatory policies of individual countries.

Europe has a long tradition in monopolistic broadcasting featuring a narrow scope of programmes. Such a role of public broadcasting service differs from the

US commercial broadcasting model in terms of strategic approach. *Prime time* and ratings have become symbols of US broadcasters around the world, as they play a central role in editorial programme policy tracking the rule "what the public wants".[33] A new dynamic media environment developing in parallel with commercialization in the 1990s led to the introducing of similar programming practices to the European broadcasting remit.

From the perspective of a TV institution, industrialization is the right answer to the challenging market: how to produce more with limited resources (production and programme capacities) in a heavily competitive market. Product standardization, expansion of production and viewing share are crucial in this transformation period. Therefore, discussions on formats, a narrow range of channels, brands and target public are paramount today. Competition in programming does not mean only more TV channels but also an enlarged scope of services (programmes) on existing channels. *The trend to around-the-clock service* (24/7)[34] dominates TV stations (Hujanen, 2002: 24). In the multi-programming environment, the quantity of services and programmes has increased without a proportionate growth of revenue. The increasing quantity of programmes and limited budgetary resources are a feature of both public and commercial broadcasters in the last decade.

The most essential demand imposed on the management of television institutions is effective performance, involving not only cost efficiency but also operational and organizational efficiency. This demand is a consequence of the new competitive media environment in which PSBs have to operate.

Assessment of the broadcasting service operation

Public-service broadcasters have undergone different institutional forms and relationships with society since their creation to the present day.

In the past century, they experienced several significant periods:

- The 1930s and 1940s are the period of experimentation and creation of television. Television took the values and mission of public radio stations.
- In the 1950s and 1960s, regular broadcasts took place under the regulatory framework, which was adopted. The number of employees in PSBs grew

33 The slogan "what the public wants" is taken from Hujanen (2002: 23), in order to distinguish between the American commercial and the European public-service broadcasting tradition. The parallel slogan of the European public-service broadcasting reads, "What the public needs".

34 Broadcasting 24 hours a day, 7 days a week.

very quickly. PSBs were the only TV organizations in most European countries. They had a monopoly position in the market because the private sector was short of resources[35]. Television stations were large and centralized organizations.
- In the 1970s, a variety of services came into full swing. New TV media players in the market incited vociferous criticism over the organizational structure and performance of the public broadcasting service.
- In the 1980s and 1990s, the move to a dual broadcasting system put obvious pressures on different areas: programming (contents), organizational structure and the role (redefinition of the role – advertising). Efforts were obviously made to improve public service efficiency. Efficiency and effectiveness needed clear criteria for their assessment.

Assessment is a process of examining whether a PSB meets its objectives and commitments. Assessing performance includes a review of commitments and objectives and an analysis of their fulfilment. Performance output comprises different degrees of measurable indicators that an organization meets. It is vital that indicators accurately relate to the organization's commitments and objectives. Criteria for accessing performance and performance output are two essential standards and assumptions used in exploring an organization's efficiency and effectiveness. Measurement of performance output is defined as a process to quantify the efficiency and effectiveness of activities, and the measurement standard for performance output is defined as a metric used to quantify efficiency and/or effectivity of activities. As for many other organizations, it is particularly important for broadcasting organizations to identify different levels of success – to determine what constitutes effectivity and what efficiency, and in what context these criteria relate to wider society.

Traditional criteria for a broadcaster's success

Regulatory and monitoring authorities define criteria for success and the "quality« of media that are particular for their national environments.[36] Criteria for the assessment of a PSB performance should consist of quantitative indicators.

---

35 Rarity of resources means a limited number of broadcasting frequencies. That is the main reason for the limited number of TV publishers.

36 An interesting quality assessment case was developed for public-service broadcasters in a research project in Japan. They defined three levels on which the quality can be developed, and four social levels or perspectives on which performance output can be assessed. These three levels are a whole media system, television channels, and

Traditional yardsticks for the assessment of PSBs' performance output are understood to be political criteria because they are defined by national regulatory policies. Individual national regulatory and monitoring authorities tried to set performance criteria already from the start. Despite its business goals, broadcasting was not treated like other industries. Due to its unique position in society, gained by its tremendous influence and involvement in social, cultural, political, and economic developments, it is treated in a particular way and continually questioned about its social role and mission. Political criteria and assessment of its performance output relate mainly to the programming, which gives broadcasting a unique position in society. Political criteria relate to measurable indicators for the assessment of performance output and are determined by regulatory provisions (media acts and laws or statutes of PSBs). These criteria are:

- number of hours of services transmitted
- output of copyright production
- informative and factual contents
- cultural contents
- children's contents
- minorities contents
- domestic (national) and foreign broadcast production
- output of the first broadcast releases compared with repeated releases
- output of national and European production
- level of universality and accessibility of services
- viewing hours

All these criteria provide a monitoring of an organization's performance. However, such a measurement of effectiveness and efficiency, in other words *assessment of performance* output, is not sufficient in today's dynamic environment. More important than the "contents" criteria are becoming the criteria for assessing a broadcaster's effectiveness and efficiency in the market. In order to achieve effective performance, it is important to provide quality services, to operate actively, successfully, and consciously in the market, and to implement modern management practices (strategic management).

This book seeks to focus on the role of political criteria, the fulfilment of particular social mission and the assessment criteria for effective and efficient

---

programme (contents and services). The four levels that can be potential quality assessors are the state, society, the public and professionals (communicators) (Ishikava and Muramatsu, 1991; McQuail, 1992).

performance. With respect to the suggested criteria, this approach resembles the approach for studying organizational effectiveness (McQuail 1992: 12). However, this study aims at a broader understanding of success. Including political and economic indicators in the study of a PSB's performance in order to evaluate its effectivity in society is a unique challenge.

The role and significance of economic criteria for performance effectiveness

European public service broadcasters are large organizations having large amounts of financial resources. In most European countries, they have much higher amounts of financial resources at their disposal than private broadcasting corporations, which seek funds in the market. Supervisory bodies are obliged to check PSBs' cost-effectiveness and the usage of large budgets.

In order to keep public support and legitimacy, it is important for an organization to ensure efficient performance, which however requires the observance of economic criteria. Economic criteria are important because they encourage the public service organization to achieve profit, and to reduce the dependence on the licence fees and other public revenues, especially in cases when it is entitled to gain revenues from advertising. The profit generated in the market enables an organization to provide the means for its development and improvement of its performance and services, and thus its survival. Efficient performance and quality services are essential criteria for an organization to be successful in a free market. Consumers (viewers) in the market value the products (programmes) irrespective of whether they are provided by private or public service broadcasters. The only consumers' criterion is the programming. Technological development and market competition also spur larger investments. Convergence of media is shown in cross-platform services and business activities. Today, offering services across different platforms has become necessary, and is part of business strategies of all media organizations.

The question that often arises is whether broadcasting is a profit or a non-profit institution. The profit-oriented concept carries a negative connotation, which public broadcasters refuse because it relates to commercial companies. There are different types of public-service organizations; the one thing they have in common is serving the public interest. A public-service company can perform profit-driven activities and choose an appropriate organizational form to serve this purpose.

The following sections present priorities and commitments imposed on the management of commercial and public broadcasting organizations.

Criteria for studying performance effectivity of commercial broadcasters

Principles of commercial broadcasters according to Piccard (2002) could be summed up in thefollowing objectives:

Maximizing the audience

- average daily ratings
  The management goal is to reach the broadest possible public; the criterion is the programme ratings. Average daily ratings are a priority issue in most broadcasters' business and programme policies.
- programme ratings
  The number of viewers of individual programmes is an important criterion in creating a broadcaster's programme policy. Apart from average daily ratings indicating the viewing throughout the day, viewing at particular times is even a more important criterion, since it refers to the ratings of individual programmes. Such indicators serve to determine future business and management strategies, because it is crucial to choose appropriate broadcast genres and contents in order to reach the widest target public.

Maximizing advertising revenues

- average revenue per viewer
  A management objective is to achieve the greatest possible income per viewer. Therefore, concentrating on the revenue per viewer is a priority of commercial TVs. While maximizing the audience focuses on the amount of the population, demography is a decisive factor for the revenue. To maximize the revenue per viewer is an essential obligation of a commercial organization. Therefore, the structure of the audience is vital.
- average income on a programme
  The amount of income derived from a particular programme is a paramount criterion in estimating the total advertising revenue. How is it possible to make a profitable programme? Maximizing advertising revenue from a particular programme is a goal of a commercial organization, which puts the focus on creating a programme that could reach the highest value for advertisers.

Maximizing profit

- average profit per broadcast hour
  Achieving the maximum profit is related to the profitability of broadcasting. An imperative criterion is the average profit per broadcast hour.

- profitability of programmes

  Television programmes have to reach a certain level of profitability. Therefore, profitability of individual programmes is a very important criterion. Hence, commercial broadcasters create management strategies, which include such programmes that would achieve a certain level of profitability.

Criteria for studying performance effectivity of public service broadcasters

Criteria for the public broadcasting service could be summed up as follows:

Political criteria for maximizing services for social, political and cultural needs

- PBS has the role of serving the public good inherently built in its inaugural mission. That imposes upon it concern for the social, political and cultural needs of the environment in which it operates.

Satisfying the public needs by efficient usage of available resources

- Effective utilization of resources by a PBS is particularly necessary due to its unique position providing advantages over commercial broadcasters (revenues from subscriptions or just exemption from the payment of frequencies).

Maximizing the audience

Concerns of public TVs' managements in respect of achieving maximum ratings should be the same as those of commercial broadcasters.

- average daily ratings
- programme ratings

Maximizing external resources

The free media market requires more and more active competition among broadcasters. Competition for the audience and advertisers has undoubtedly increased, and public-service broadcasters are going to play a crucial role in this game.

- maximizing advertising revenues
- maximizing sales of programmes[37]

37 The operation of the BBC deriving a large share of its revenue from the sales of programmes and services in Europe proves that quality programmes can and should be sold to other national markets, and that the language barriers can be overcome.

Seeking additional sources of funding and expansion of products and services across international markets should be a priority in management strategies of public-service broadcasters.

Maximizing efficiency

- efficient utilization of resources
  In Europe, two different systems of organizational structures are most frequent: a flexible and reasonably flat one on one hand and a cumbersome and hierarchical one on the other. The latter is typical of most public-service broadcasters in Europe. The dynamic media market requires a flexible organizational structure enabling efficient use of resources.
- producing reserves
  The period of economic crisis has shown the revenue from the advertising market to be very volatile. That is why TV organizations have faced the need to produce reserves in order to safeguard themselves against potential dangers of the market. Predictions of annual budgets are not so accurate anymore as they used to be in the 1990s. Additional reserves also mean the ability to invest in new technologies and new services, which can supply potential revenues.

In all national environments, regulatory bodies observe the political criteria adopted in monitoring public broadcasting services. That is not merely an evaluation but a control over the performance of public broadcasting services. There are some traditional criteria for monitoring public-service broadcasters that are commonly used by most European regulatory bodies. Piccard (2002) also presented criteria for assessing performance output with the intention of promoting efficiency of public broadcasting services. This book deals with the management of broadcasting organization in all aspects. Therefore, both the political and economic criteria were observed in exploring performance output of public broadcasters.

Common economic criteria for studying performance effectivity of public and commercial media

This book sheds light on the role of economic criteria for the assessment of PBS performance, since only observance of these standards can ensure that a public service broadcaster is successful in the market and fulfils the role and mission entrusted to it on its establishment. Like commercial media organizations, public media organizations can also be effective if they observe criteria: of market share, productivity, financing, and management. *Marketing criteria for performance output mean a sufficient viewing share. Criteria of productivity* mean output per employee, value added per employee and productivity of capital. *Financial criteria* for performance output mean concern for the revenue growth, financial results and the value of assets. Management criteria mean concern for reinvestments and expenditures, as well as for innovation and seeking new business opportunities.

Market-share criteria

Not long ago, the market success of public broadcasting services was obvious, and defenders of public-service broadcasters did not pay any attention to this criterion. That could be attributed to the stable market shares[38] of public media in the middle 1990s. Commercial media that appeared in the market have contributed new criteria for performance effectivity. Public-service broadcasters were not capable of advocating their unique role in society anymore while losing their market shares. Their 100 per cent market share was critically reduced.

The issue of market share and success in the market, which is connected to the question of how to retain a role, significance and survival in the market, has become the primary generator of all media performance, not only private but also the public service. The role of the public broadcasting service is defined at the national level, which means that its role in the market and its market share are also subject to discussions at the national level.

We hypothesize that public-service broadcasters do not have the same target audience as their commercial competitors. They strive for the largest market share possible; however, they seek demographic and time gaps. Results based on current relations among European TV publishers show that consumption of television services does not increase in proportion to the quantity of contents. That is due to the viewing time, which does not increase in proportion to the quantity of services offered. Excessive supply of programmes and services results in the segmentation of public and increased competition among TV publishers.

Results gained by calculations of actual market share and expected average viewing share (based on the number of active TV publishers) indicate the

38 Market share means viewing share for a television programme. This research concentrates more on the market share than on the ratings since the market share can give a more real picture on the viewing and the position of a TV channel. The share indicates the number of viewers or households with switched on receivers watching a certain programme. The rating indicates a percentage of individuals or households of the whole population.

performance output of TV organizations. Piccard (2002) studied the role of European PSBs and used the suggested formula as a criterion of performance output. His analysis results show that public broadcasting services retain their powerful role in national markets.

Criteria of productivity

Criteria of productivity relating to the revenue per employee can be used for broadcasters that are funded by commercial income. Employees who are directly engaged in commercial activities (or all employees) can serve as a criterion for assessing performance effectivity of commercial activities. Many public broadcasting services obtain a larger part of their income from other sources (state subsidies and subscriptions) rather than from the market. That is why their criteria of productivity differ from those of market-driven broadcasters. Performing in the market (financing solely from advertising) provides criteria for assessing productivity and performance effectivity. However, these indicators are not transparent in the case of funding from the budget.

The number of programme hours per employee or the number of produced programme per employee indicates the broadcaster's productivity. Monitoring of the performance and productivity are necessary tasks to achieve effective performance output.

Financial criteria

The primary management task in a TV organization is monitoring of financial performance. Financial criteria mean monitoring revenue growth, financial results, debts, and the value of assets. These criteria are reasonable for TV organizations that are financed by advertising revenues. The growth of revenues resulting from all commercial activities (also selling of programmes) is an important criterion, which indicates the trends of media market behaviour.[39]

Monitoring the value of assets and observing market trends is also very important, since European public-service broadcasters are still gigantic institutions operating with large financial resources and fixed assets. Comparison of the value of assets between the private and public service broadcasters in Europe indicates that the value of assets of PSBs is twice as large. That is also a reason why good husbandry is becoming an important obligation in public service organizations.

---

39 Selling programmes and licences for programmes has become the key activity of many broadcasters and publishers in Europe.

Management criteria

It is vitally important that both public service and private media organizations be managed so that they can successfully compete in the market. To be competitive in free media market means to be *economically competitive.*

Management of a media organization has to cope with modernization of a medium (modernization of organizational structure, production, product line, and productivity). Focusing on modernization and introduction of new technologies is the most important management task in today's turbulent media market. New technologies enable higher-quality services, introduction of new services, higher productivity, and improvement of the whole media performance. Capital investments in technology are part of the management strategy, which affects the whole organization. Appropriate investments are an important criterion for the performance output, effectiveness of the management and consequently the broadcaster.

Successful management depends on effective marketing which the result is of precisely and efficiently designed corporate strategies. Market segmentation focuses on individual markets aiming at reaching particular target publics. Market positioning focuses on the shaping of a clear corporate identity, and its differentiation, to make it distinctive in the competitive market. Promoting trademarks is an important strategy for linking media organizations with particular features of their product (programme). (Albarran, 2000: 208)

Innovation and creativity are essential features of broadcasting in each development phase, from its creation until today. Creativity in television genres receded into the background in the last decade because creativity in using new technologies took its place. In addition, talents focus their creativity on new services, new technologies, and the use of technological and human potentials. Innovation in production and the product line is most valued in the market today. Research and improvements of technologies and services, and the development of new products and services are based on the creativity and innovativeness of a media organization. An important criterion for assessing performance output is the degree of innovativeness and creativity achieved in a media organization.

Economic criteria for performance output, consisting of market share criteria, financial criteria, criteria of productivity and management criteria, are the key criteria for assessing effectivity of corporate management strategies. These criteria enable an overall assessment of the economical behaviour in a TV organization.

6. Analysis of the Management of a Hybrid TV Model

This chapter presents and examines management strategies of the mixed public-commercial management system of the Channel Four Television Corporation. In a thorough assessment of the corporation's performance output and hypotheses, traditional and economic criteria showing effectivity of its management strategies were applied. The research aims at finding out how a mixed management model works, without seeking advantages or disadvantages of different management models.

Channel 4, fulfilling a particular social mission as a public broadcasting service and at the same time operating as a commercial broadcaster in the free market, is an interesting model for studying the performance of broadcasting service. Such a type of organization is a challenge for the management, requiring coordination and reconciliation of conflicts between the different interests of a unique social mission and commercial effectivity. However, its outcomes prove the mixed management practice to have a chance of survival in Europe.

Political criteria versus economic criteria

Public service broadcasters operate as part of social systems in many countries, and they are governed by national regulatory authorities. Regulatory bodies supervise and monitor how they fulfil their social mission and define framework standards for their performance. Usually, they concentrate only on a review of programme contents. Therefore, for categories that escape clear definition (such as the quality of contents and the educational nature of contents) an attempt is made to classify them in quantitatively defined categories. Traditional criteria for performance denote criteria for achieving the social mission, which, together with an "appropriate" quantity of "appropriate" contents, can safeguard the public broadcasting service in different social systems.

This study adds to these political criteria a hypothesis that such an institution has to contribute to the economic welfare of society too. Hence, economic criteria are also included in the evaluation process, helping to make a complete picture of the functioning of public-commercial Channel Four Television Corporation. For a more transparent study of performance output, assessment criteria were defined for use in presenting particular areas of governance. The survey focuses on a case study, which is autonomous and unique. That resulted in an independent rather than a comparative analysis. A comparative study into various similar institutions would not serve the purpose, because the mixed management practice of the Channel Four Television Corporation is a unique example.

Economic criteria are appropriate when analysing performance output of different organizations or comparing performance output of a single organization through different periods. The central question of the research is how Channel Four Television Corporation achieves an economic effectiveness and how it meets economic criteria for performance output, while it is also committed to fulfilment of a particular social mission.

Political criteria

Channel 4 is supervised once a year, in former times by the ITC, and now by Ofcom. According to their reports, Channel 4 provides a sufficient quantity of news and current affairs, and meets provisions related to educational, school, religious and multicultural programmes. It has to transmit a certain percentage of originated production and must not exceed the specified amount of repeats. It shall provide a specified quantity of European production and a specified share of contents produced outside London. Since 2001, it must also observe the provision requiring a specified number of hours with subtitled contents. Criteria on the quantity of programmes to be supplied by independent production companies are also very precise.

TV contents

Monitoring of the PSBs' performance output most often focuses on checking the adequacy of contents. The fulfilment of a special social mission is evaluated by checking whether all criteria related to the contents are met. Channel 4 has to provide yearly 208 hours of news, 208 hours of current affairs[40], 364 hours of educational, 330 hours of school, 52 hours of religious and 156 hours of multicultural programmes.

According to data, Channel 4 meets the required amount of specified broadcast hours.[41] Moreover, it seems that Channel 4 exceeds the prescribed quantity of socially relevant contents. That is particularly obvious with the school,

40 Current affairs programme includes the following genres: current events, economy and politics.

41 The quantity of hours is a measurable category. The category »relevant quality« or »programme of high quality" is difficult to evaluate.

educational and multicultural programmes where amounts significantly exceed minimum required quantities.

The tables (attached in the end) show TV contents provided over the recent period and indicate its programming policy. It seems that the media market has prompted Channel 4 to broadcast more sports contents. One of the reasons for doing so is also the cost of programmes. Quality broadcasts such as arts and documentaries are more expensive than entertainment programmes.

Diversity of programme genres

Programming is the most important tool of the Channel Four Television Corporation, since scheduling of different genres across the broadcast time and within prime time is crucial for a programme to be successful. The ITC requires diversity of programming throughout the broadcast day, and especially during the peak time between 6 and 11 PM. Besides quantities of socially relevant contents during the peak time compared to the whole-day programming, diversity of genres is also subject to control. Channel 4 has a more extensive choice of broadcast genres (ten different genres in prime time) compared to other broadcast programmes: long-running series, comedies, entertainment shows, quiz and game shows, sport, peak-time news, broadcasts on leisure, science, medicine, people and curiosities and modern music.

Other provisions of the programme

ITC monitors the achievement of required quantities of originated contents, subtitled and European contents, repeats and production outside London. At least 60 percent of the Channel 4's programme has to be originated or purchased for Channel 4, and at least 70 percent of originated programme must be broadcast in prime time. The Corporation must ensure that repeats do not exceed 40 percent of all broadcasts, and 20 percent in prime time. The contents produced by independent production companies must reach at least a share of 25 percent in all Channel 4's broadcasts. Programming of European origin[42] must comprise at least 50 percent of all broadcasts, not including news, sports transmissions and advertising. The Corporation has to increase the amount of subtitled contents. The broadcasting licence commits Channel 4 to devote at least 30 percent of its programming budget to production houses outside London. That makes the Corporation collaborate with as many production houses as possible. In addi-

42 European production also includes the domestic (British) production.

tion, it encourages the growth of the creative sector, not only in the capital city but also throughout the UK.

The growth of the independent production industry in the UK was the main reason for the creation of Channel 4. The growth is due to the scope of collaboration with independent production houses. Channel 4 broadcasts much more programme from independent production than its largest commercial rival ITV does. However, it has reduced it compared to the 1980s and 1990s.

Programme strategy of Channel 4 based on political criteria

The latest ITC reports reveal that all providers of terrestrial channels have reduced their scope of programmes, and that individual socially relevant contents appear more rarely in prime time. That obviously means that many programmes for minority target groups have found their place outside prime time. A decline in the genres of art and current affairs is most evident (almost 40 percent) with commercial broadcasters.

Factual[43] contents including educational programmes have mainly retained their share, while news increased its airtime on Channel 4 and on the other two commercial broadcasters. Data also show that religious broadcasts have found their place in prime time again.

The percentage of entertainment shows has increased in prime time as expected. Drama contents have decreased in quantity, while light programmes increased in all commercial programming and on Channel 4 by over two percent.

The larger part of independent production broadcasts is scheduled in prime time. Purchases of programmes (mostly movies) have reduced substantially on all commercial channels. Channel 4, which was considered as a »movie« channel a few years ago, records a considerable drop in purchased film contents.

News has remained a recognizable brand of Channel 4 since it continues its strongly-established daily news programme (55 minutes at 7 PM). Longer news also gives a chance for an alternative perspective of international developments and an analytical approach.

In sports programming, Channel 4 has oriented towards specialized contents such as horseracing and cricket as distinctive British sports. Channel 4's diversity compared to other broadcasters also demonstrates in genres shown in prime time. In prime time, it broadcasts a larger share of drama and sports contents.

---

43 *Factual* are the following genres: educational and religious broadcasts, broadcasts on science, art, history and documentaries.

A change of the programme strategy became most evident after the abolition of the "funding formula", when Channel 4 started to act and compete independently in the market. Then, it also began attracting a broader audience in prime time. The biggest change affected genres, precisely the ratios among genres. The amount of broadcasts, however, did not change. The 167 hours per week broadcast in 1997 remained the same as in 2001. News and current affairs increased by two hours per week by 2001 compared to 1997. On the other hand, documentaries took much less airtime, occupying 10 hours a week in 1997 but only about six hours in 2001. Educational contents recorded a notable increase (7 hours a week more in 2001 than in 1997). That was at the expense of a significant decrease of children's contents (7 hours a week less in 2001 compared to 1997). Entertainment contents occupied much more airtime in 2001 than in 1997 (increase by one-third). These broadcasts filled a quarter of weekly airtime (39 hours and 54 minutes).

Studying management of Channel 4, it is necessary to take account of political criteria determining measurable broadcast categories (hours), because they are essential to retaining the broadcasting licence. For that reason, the standards for the observance of the public interest were included in the study of Channel 4 within the specified period.

Economic criteria

Market-share criteria

Market-share criteria are an essential tool in exploring the economic effectivity of an organization. Public service broadcasters, too, have a growing concern about their performance effectivity in a free market and thereby providing a planned market share. The Channel 4's market share was examined by observing its ratings of the entire programme and individual programmes and by studying demography, where attention was paid to the relationship between the target and the reached public.

Channel 4 was created to serve the needs of various minorities in society. »It will provide a full spectrum of views and opinions so that all will watch it at times and not all of them all the time." (Isaacs, 1989: 19–20) The ratings and the scope of genres show that Channel 4 competes for audience with the programmes of BBC 2. Furthermore, comparisons of viewing shares between Channel 4 and other broadcasters prove the ratings of Channel 4 to be stable. The biggest jump makes satellite and cable channels that emerged in the media market only a decade ago.

A different picture appears when taking account of all terrestrial broadcasting organizations, including all their subsidiary digital programmes. All terrestrial broadcasting corporations also provide digital programmes (cable, satellite and terrestrial); therefore, the entire broadcasting family should be taken into account.

Data on the number of watch hours show that the quantity of hours devoted to TV has not significantly changed. The only interesting thing is the change in ratios and shares of the viewing time spent for individual programmes. Viewing hours for cable and satellite programmes grew, but declined for the BBC and ITV programmes. Channel 4 has kept the same average daily viewing.

Ratings (specialized and mass programmes)

Reviews of ratings offer very relevant information that could help in designing programme strategies. Channel 4 was considered a »movie channel« at the beginning, because it was the first UK channel that provided a wide range of the world's film production. Its orientation towards film diminished in time, when provisions for public broadcasting service concerning its unique social mission became more stringent. Despite that, it retained a sufficient portion of film contents with high enough ratings.

Analyses of the most-watched shows on the main Channel 4 showed that American movies did not guarantee the highest ratings any longer. That is why Channel 4 started broadcasting more British production and different genres (documentaries) over the years. In the recent time, the most popular shows were those containing various genres in a single product, and thereby attracting different target audiences.[44] Such broadcasts also provide higher viewing by the targeted audience.

Demography (reached and target public)

The picture of ratings gets another dimension when looking at the population watching different programmes. The advertising market treats each public group in a different way. Market research focuses on the following population groups: housewives, adults, the ABC1[45] adults, the C2DE[46] adults, adults between 16 and

44 An example of such kind of mixing of genres is documentary-entertainment-educational shows (broadcasts on interesting historical discoveries and shows about cooking and leisure).

45 The group is defined based on education, employment, status, and age. The ABC1 adults group is the most demanding, market-oriented group of consumers. These are more highly educated, wealthy, higher classes (A – upper middle class, B – middle class, C1 – lower middle class).

46 The C2DE group includes the lower classes with lower income and lower education (C2 – skilled workers, D – workers, E – people with the lowest income, seniors).

34 years of age, adults between 35 and 54 years of age, adults aged over 55 years, men, women, children. The Channel 4's target groups are adults between 16 and 34 years of age and the ABC1 adults. That is the most demanding audience with high education, responsible positions at work and high salaries. According to data, the main Channel 4 recorded higher ratings by the ABC1 population.

Management strategies according to market-share criteria

Channel 4 clearly focused on attracting minority groups in its early years. Its strategy changed after the abolition of the »funding formula« aiming at stabilizing (or even increasing) the audience of all categories. Striving to meet the PBS's commitments and achieve sufficient ratings and thereby at the same time advertisers, it implemented flexible programming.

Channel Four Television Corporation tries to bridge the gap in the media market. Its strategic programme direction tracks the goal of providing high-quality contents to attract "quality" minority groups. Hence, it reoriented its programme from a film channel towards a channel of predominantly British production, mixed genres and a large proportion of documentaries. The ratings by the 55 +, children and 35–54 target groups have not increased as much as by the ABC1 category. Furthermore, the male audience increased while the female decreased.

The viewing results could be considered from various perspectives. Firstly, the number of viewers declined a bit over the last five years. Secondly, the audience has stabilized compared to that of other large terrestrial broadcasters (BBC and ITV) where it declined due to the rise of satellite and cable programmes. Thirdly, Channel 4 together with all its subsidiary programmes increased its ratings compared to the BBC and ITV programmes (including digital). The market-share analysis is presumed to be correct when it also includes households with the satellite and cable connections. The study concentrates on the management of the entire Channel Four Television Corporation and not merely on the Channel 4 programme. Therefore, it is necessary to pay attention to the performance and effectiveness of all organizational units, including those that transmit digital programmes.

Criteria of productivity

Performance output is an important criterion besides the broadcasting programme and services as core activities. Providing programme contents and services is a core activity of all broadcasters. Their programme productivity is measured by the size of their human resources »capital«. Broadcasters acquiring the majority of financial resources from advertising can measure commercial success by the size of the human resources they use to ensure income.

Productivity of an organization is subject to its employment policy. A few essential characteristics concerning HR management significantly affect the productivity.

Revenue per employee

Advertising and sponsorship revenues have grown all the time. The number of employees increased in both the Corporation and the departments of sales and market research. Comparing the amount of income and the number of the corporation's HR force cannot show a complete picture. The fact is that the performance of the entire corporation depends on the effectiveness of advertising and its revenues. However, only the marketing department earns advertising income.

The quantity of transmissions per employee

Since 1997, the number of employees in the Corporation increased. On the other hand, the amount of broadcast hours on the main Channel 4 did not grow significantly (from 8734 to 8760) but the costs of programmes did. An average amounted to 14 broadcast hours per employee in 1997 and only 8 hours in 2001.

Initial investments in additional services and programmes of 4Ventures were enormous. Therefore, it is reasonable to concentrate only on the productivity of the main Channel 4. The quantity of transmissions per employee decreased; the ratio of costs to the number of employees, however, did not significantly change over recent years, because both programme costs and the number of employees increased.

Management strategies according to criteria of productivity

During the period 1997–2010, there was a significant growth in the employee force, especially in the marketing department (sales of advertising airtime) and in the departments for procurement and selection of programme contents. Productivity of advertising activities declined due to changed circumstances in the advertising market. Productivity in the production and broadcasting has dropped by 17 percent (in terms quantity of broadcast hours). That accounts for higher costs of programmes, both of British and foreign production. At the same time, there was a substantial influx of employees into the Corporation, especially into 4Ventures, which however is not committed to specific and precise provisions on the necessary quantity of contents, genres and services.

The Corporation did not opt for restrictive measures of employment, which could have undermined the quality of the programme. Neither did it increase the number of broadcast hours. Instead, it retained a certain amount of programmes, which, however, resulted in a 37 percent increase in programme costs. The productivity of Channel Four Television Corporation seems to have declined because of investments in new technologies and higher programme costs. The Corporation followed a strategy of reducing programme costs per employee. That forced it to dedicate a larger budget to individual contents and to spend less airtime for them compared to previous years. Compromises in quantity were necessary to maintain the quality of contents.

Earnings from advertising and sponsorship were not equally effective at all corporate levels. Neither has the increase in the employee force in 4Ventures over the past two years brought additional advertising income to the Corporation yet. A comparison between the number of employees and the amount of advertising revenue shows a disproportion between the growth of employees and the income earned. The number of workers on the main programme related to the earnings made from this programme reveals that productivity remained the same. The most significant indicator is productivity of the commercial sector, which did not significantly drop over the period of this study.

The productivity of the commercial sector measured by the share of advertising revenue remained unchanged, while the productivity of the entire Corporation recorded a slight drop, because the employee force grew faster than the advertising income. The amount of broadcasts related to the number of employees declined, while the costs of the programme per employee on the main Channel 4 remained unchanged, which indicates a reduced productivity. If one also considers the changes in the global market, which contributed to increased programme costs (the rights) and reduced advertising revenue, it is evident that productivity trends remained at the same level through all the years.

To measure productivity of programmes based on their quantity and cost is quite simple. However, it is much more complex to measure the quality and performance of contents. That is why such productivity can be observed only partially in creating broadcasting strategies. Management conducted according to preset productivity criteria provides only a framework for creative potential, while its value has to be measured by other indicators.

Financial criteria

Channel 4 launched a completely new era of financial management in 1999. Then, it made its last payment of surplus income earned in the advertising market under the »funding formula«. Since then, it had to focus on earning sufficient income in the market to fund its business activities and the development of new programmes, since it ceased to be entitled to any subventions.

Growth of income

Conditions in the British advertising market in the early 1990s differed significantly from those at the end of the century. Until 1997, there were only two broadcasters – ITV and Channel 4 – earning advertising revenue in the market. Channel 5 appeared in 1997 and increased its advertising share by the end of 2001. At the end of the 1990s, satellite and cable channels penetrated the advertising market. Broadcasting organizations (ITV, Channel 4) opted for enormous investments in state-of-the-art digital programmes.

The income of Channel Four Television Corporation grew over the period studied. Parallel to it, the costs of broadcasting and marketing (disproportionately) rose and thereby profits decreased.

Advertising

Advertising and sponsorship are the core source of the Channel 4's income. Advertising revenue reflects its programme strategy, targeting relevant audiences and favourable recognition of its trademark.

Channel 4's advertising income increased after the abolition of the funding formula. (In 1997, it amounted £ 513.4 million. After the suspension of the funding formula in 1999, it increased to £ 600.5 million, and in 2001 to £ 619.4 million.) While it looks as if this is not a significant increase, it is critical that its advertising share in the market did not decline.

In 1997, Channel 4 acquired a 21.5 percent advertising market share and raised it by two percent in 2001. Thus, other commercial broadcasters suffered losses in advertising market shares.

New sources of income

The advertising market at the end of the 1990s proved to be an extremely unstable source of funding, especially for traditional media. New technologies and the recession in the global marketplace had unfavourable consequences for all advertising markets. Despite the advertising market share remaining stable also in the most hectic years, Channel 4 had to seek new ways of funding and strengthening of its trademark.

Channel Four Television Corporation is a multiplatform and multichannel media company; it provides free and pay-per-view channels, online and mobile services, the film and production activities, publishing activities (print) and a subdivision for international distribution. A new organizational structure efficiently joined all other commercial activities of Channel 4. They cover pay-TV programmes, sales of various products (books, CDs), mobile telephony services (voting, games), international distribution and sales of its programmes. Investments in new technologies affected the costs of the entire Corporation.

Management strategies according to financial criteria
According to data, the advertising market share increased with the suspension of the funding formula (as opposed to the largest commercial broadcaster ITV) and thereby the crucial corporate income (advertising and sponsorship). Channel 4 expected a higher revenue from advertising, but they did not anticipate such turmoil in the economy as affected the British (and global) advertising market. It is important to highlight that they succeeded in fulfilling their public mission (political criteria) even though they earned their financial resources in the market and did not seek additional public funding (national grants, subscription). The reason was that Channel 4 was capable of reaching the audience that attracted advertisers.

Funding the Corporation exclusively by advertising income dictated quick action and response to the market trends, social change and satisfaction of target audiences. The Corporation responded to the growing modernization and competition by new and complementary products. Volatile revenues earned in the market require constant analyzing of its trends and responding to its requirements. On the other hand, a secure funding base (licence fee) does not impose any immediate business and programme measures. That is why measures, which have been postponed, require much more effort and are hard to execute. Channel 4 needs to adjust and regulate its financial and programme policy more often than it would in the case of a secure funding. Its existence as a public-commercial service depends upon quick and adequate responses to the market.

Channel 4 is an innovative corporation using a variety of platforms and introducing new technologies into the existing (traditional) services. That guideline, supported by a dynamic and fast-developing British media environment, led to the decision to implement new technologies at the turn of the century. It resulted in enormous investments and thereby the decrease in corporate profits. The results of the market effectiveness (ratings) suggest that conducting business through additional platforms is necessarily also for PBSs. Only in such a way can they keep sufficient viewing and consequently a large enough advertising share.

Management criteria

Effective management affects all levels of an organization. It results in successful business outcomes, implementation of efficient marketing strategies, smart investments in new technologies and an effective organizational structure.

Promotion of programmes and the broadcasting channel
The design and recognition of a broadcasting trademark is imperative in an environment with a multitude of channels, which strive to attract audience by their uniqueness in programming and attitude towards the population.

Channel Four Television Corporation paid particular attention to its trademark, which differentiated it from all other channels. The Channel 4 trademark is well established. It is recognizable in denoting not only the broadcasting channel but also other products such as events, programmes and publications. Channel 4 had the following characteristics at its launching:

- commercial financial resources
- national services[47]
- publisher rather than producer
- consistent supporter of independent production
- provider of "quality" contents and news in prime time
- provider of innovative products and services
- provider of contents for minority groups
- flexible and easily manageable programming

All of these features have contributed to a recognizable and successful position of Channel 4 right from the beginning. Channel 4's trademark denotes a creative, cultural and innovative channel over the whole period. In the 1990s, it denoted a minority channel standing out from the crowd. In recent times, however, it marks devotion to innovation and particularity of its state-of-the-art products and services. In the 1980s and 1990s, it experimented with various cultural practices and creativity of contents. Today, it implements creativity in technology and exploits challenges of new media platforms. New media platforms mingle creativity and innovation of contents with technology, blurring the border between them.

Devotion to innovation vindicates the exploration of new platforms, which Channel 4 succeeds in using more effectively and creatively than its rivals.[48] In the early period, creativity and innovation were expressed by programme contents (for minorities, art and documentaries and other marginalized contents). Today, they are implemented in technological developments, synergy effects between traditional and new media, and in new cultural practices. The activities of Channel 4 show its striving for a targeted market share and not being satisfied with a marginal position.

---

47 Channel 4 held a national frequency licence, while the ITV and 14 regional broadcasters held regional frequency licences, which could cover the entire national territory only after their association.

48 Big Brother and other reality shows are examples of the use and exploration of different media platforms.

Pressures of the free market forced Channel 4 to change its strategy. Now, it commits to reaching a broader scope of public and does not insist on satisfying only small target groups anymore. The market-oriented approach also contributed to a more active promotion of its trademark and products compared to the early period, when ratings were not primary concern.

Organizational structure

The organizational structure of Channel Four Television Corporation resembles more those of private commercial broadcasters than of the European PBSs. Channel 4 was established as a publisher and it implemented a unique organizational model already at the beginning. This status was substantially backed by the independent production industry too.

Channel 4 practises a flat organizational structure, unlike the hierarchical structures of large PBSs. (Figure: Organizational chart of Channel 4). Departments are independent, being accountable for observing the planned budget and reporting to the executive director. All other activities besides the broadcasting programme on Channel 4 (such as digital TV programmes, interactive TV, Internet-based services, products, telephone service, production equipment) are gathered together in the 4Ventures Company. 4Ventures uses the resources of joint departments (finance, research, public relations). Independent departments follow the corporate culture as expressed in the corporate statutes.

The Organization has to provide enough autonomy to the departments, which means interrelations should not be too tight. Such an approach makes it flexible and quickly responsive to market requirements. Its management structure is much less hierarchical than the BBC's and ITV's.

Publisher – producer

Channel 4 was created primarily as a publisher rather than a »typical« broadcaster. It buys, edits and broadcasts programmes produced outside the Corporation. It is obliged to follow traditional criteria committing it to broadcast a large amount of contents bought from independent production companies. These provisions dictate a large portion of contents satisfying the public good. The status as a publisher allows the broadcaster to set up a rational management structure without hiring expensive creative human resources, but rather by project cooperation with independent production companies. Such an arrangement encourages the British creative industry, which could not develop before Channel 4 came on air, since BBC and ITV used only their own resources.

Recruitment of expensive creative human resources is obviously much less effective without previous in-depth knowledge of their performance. That is especially true for the broadcasting programme, which requires project work for a particular (short or long) time. The publisher's advantage over a typical broadcaster is its more efficient programming. That is due to its management structure, because an independent production company takes responsibility for the quality of a programme and manages the contractual budget too. The Channel 4 publishing company makes a request for a particular programme, indicating all the characteristics (quality, price). On this basis, it fixes ratings and the value of the programme. Contracts stipulate the predetermined characteristics, which commissioned programmes have to meet at the responsibility of independent production companies. Good management of publishing activities is characterized in particular by a clear vision and a choice of a quality producer.

Compared to the classical broadcasting industry, the publisher does not hire creative human resources before the start of projects. Instead, it includes them in a planned programme project that it orders with a production house.

Channel 4 also does not pay costs of expensive equipment that is constantly changing and losing its value due to technological developments. Technical and production equipment are the burdens of production companies, which collaborate with many broadcasters and publishers and incorporate their costs in individual projects.

The problem that often occurs in publishing activity is copyrights that a production company can keep. Channel 4 records register almost half of the programmes, the copyrights of which are held not only by Channel 4, but also by production houses.

Most independent production houses agree that Channel Four Television Corporation is the only one in the market that provides unique genres (non-traditional). In addition, it decides more quickly on risky projects and experiments in the programme more than other broadcasters do.[49]

Management strategies according to management criteria

Governance of Channel 4 based on successful management output coping with the positioning and promotion of its trademark, organizational structure and investments in new technologies. The study of the positioning and character of the Channel 4's trademark shows a clear strategy for its recognition. Channel 4 has established itself by being innovative, multicultural, progressive, creative and

---

49 Endemol UK scored the highest place among the European production houses, amongst other things thanks to the courage and willingness to take risks with the project Big Brother.

diverse through all its periods, but always in a different way. In the early period, diversity, innovation and creativity were apparent in programme contents. At the turn of the millennium, innovation and creativity moved to the technological level by combining traditional and new media and launching new state-of-the-art services. In addition, the Corporation was also creative in seeking financial resources.

The pursuit of technological innovation is the driving force of the media development. That is exactly what Channel 4 did. It tested new approaches and started providing new services. It was the first to launch many new services in the British media market, which required enormous investments in the use of new technologies. Many of the investments have not made a substantial income by today. However, the corporate top management believes investments to be the only possible way to ensure a powerful role for Channel 4 in the future media market.

A hierarchical, bureaucratic organizational structure may be not efficient in a creative market such as broadcasting. A rapid response to the market is possible only in case of relatively independent departments and a flat management structure. Channel 4 responds more quickly because it is more flexible than ITV and BBC. Its flexibility intensified in 2001, when all additional services apart from the main broadcasting channel were gathered together in 4Ventures. That also caused a further flattening of the management structure.

The position of Channel 4 as a publisher is often crucial for its efficiency and effectivity. Independent production companies produce programmes ordered by Channel 4 (in terms of quality and price), and are responsible for their success in the market. At the same time, the creative human potential is tied to the projects produced by an independent production company. Channel 4 does not hire any expensive human resources that would "wait" for the projects to start. Such a kind of arrangement is paramount for the social mission of broadcasting, which acts as a catalyst for creativity in society producing a broad scope of creative contents for the market in collaboration with independent producers.

The chapter brings the results of the analysis of the governance of Channel Four Television Corporation according to political and economic criteria. Political criteria are presented as requirements by regulatory bodies imposed on Channel 4 for the realization of public interest. Economic criteria comprise achievement of market share, utilization of resources (productivity), financial management and governance of Channel 4. The analysis of Channel 4's management examined the corporate strategic direction and assessed the effectiveness of corporate managerial practices.

The positioning of Channel 4 in the British media market

Comparisons of Channel 4 with incumbent public service BBC are interesting. Both are public broadcasters; however, they differentiate in three essential characteristics. The BBC's only funding source is subscription, while Channel 4 earns all its income in the advertising market. The BBC submits itself to its own regulatory body (earlier to the BBC Board of Governors and now the BBC Trust), while Channel 4 is regulated by an external regulatory body. The BBC and Channel 4 have different target audiences. BBC is committed to the principle of universality, while Channel 4 seeks specific population groups that attract advertisers. In addition, they differentiate in their social responsibility. BBC has to provide news, educational and entertainment programmes of high standards, offer contents that interest local and national publics, and ensure accuracy and impartiality of information. Channel 4 plays a complementary role in relation to ITV (and BBC). It is committed to provide innovative and experimental programmes in terms of form and content.

Economic uncertainty in the British media market is a result of the growing competition, a downturn in advertising revenue, threats of economic recession and increased investments in new state-of-the-art services on different platforms. Income from licences for pay-per-view channels has become an important source for developing new business models to earn additional revenue. In such a turmoil in the market and in view of the necessary investments in technological development, public broadcasters have to find a balance between their commitment to social mission and their survival in the market. The situation at the turn of millennium has cultural and social implications: a multicultural society with erosion of essential features of national cultures, changed ways of watching multi-channel TV (time lags), and consequently fragmentation and segmentation of the public (Dodd and Stevenson, 2001). However, it is not yet clear how far and in what form these changes will develop in the future. Television seems to be an exception because its customers are reluctant to use new technologies, feeling uncertain about their advantages and disadvantages, and fearing their early obsolescence and high costs.

The British PBSs are forced to be quite flexible and adaptable to the challenges of new technologies. The history of Channel Four Television Corporation is unique. Since abolition of the "funding formula" in 1997, it keeps investing its profits into the development of new services and higher costs of programmes, especially those from the United States. The employee force has increased in number and expansion of new services has continued: two pay-per-view channels, new Internet and interactive services. In 2001, 4Ventures gathered all commercial activities under one roof. The Corporation achieved notable financial results in the 1990s. At the turn of millennium, however, it had to deal with redundancies and cuts in budgets.

New services with growing and diversified income

Faced with a decline in advertising revenues, Channel 4 found an economic rationale in earning income from licence fees, sponsorship, sales of rights (copyrights), and sales of interactive and Internet services. An orientation towards commercialism seems to be an imperative in ensuring income to meet its social mission and develop new state-of-the-art services. Business-oriented performance does not contradict the corporate mission.

There is greater concern, however, over competition among platforms, which affects the stability of Channel 4. On the other hand, a shift towards production and distribution activities gives a competitive edge.

Maintaining and increasing viewing shares

An important goal in promoting new technologies and new services is a rise in ratings for the primary channel. The share of households with multichannel connections is now a main criterion of success on the British broadcasting market, since it seems to be an important indicator in the future.

Spreading and strengthening of the trademark

New services aim at spreading and strengthening principal values of the Channel 4's trademark. In a multichannel digital remit, a unique and favourably well-recognized trademark is vitally important.

Corporate internal documents assign to the Channel 4's trademark the following ten characteristics: state-of-the-art, innovative, ready to take the risk, free, new perspectives, business-oriented, creative and exquisite, quality production, let the viewers decide. These values are often quoted in strategic directions of Channel 4. Diversity, which was a buzzword of the public sector over an extended period, reads differently in its statement:

> "Channel 4 believes in freedom of the individual and wants to promote diversity of opinions and freedom of expression." (Channel 4 reports)

The meaning of diversity often differs in theory and practice. The public broadcasting service denotes it as diversity of programmes, genres, cultural diversity and programmes for and about minority groups.

Shares of demographic groups

Public TVs have to face the fact that the concept of a PBS has small significance for British youth, since the audience under 35 years of age finds the multichannel television more attractive. Thus, demographic indicators were a significant factor in the implementation of new digital services on Channel 4: with the aim to reach young viewers and attract their attention to the vision of the public service Channel 4. A striving to rejuvenate the audience is reflected in the »innovative entertainment" shows on Channel 4:

At the same time, a large concern for the young audience has to be balanced with a commitment to universality as a fundamental principle of the public service: to attract a substantial and varied audience.

Adapting to the new pay-per-view economy

There are important reasons for deciding on the new pay-per-view economic model and the need to stay in touch with customers and new technologies. The driving force is the fact that pay-per-view economy is the future. Channel 4 has to accept this reality and respond adequately to the market developments.

The pay-per-view economy follows its own principles. American programmes sell rights of pay-free TV programmes together with pay-TV packages. Channel 4 pursues the practice of selling pay-TV contents at any opportunity.

Cross platforms and interactive potential

New services of Channel Four Television Corporation provide cross-media and cross-platform usage and interactive services, these being the inevitable and priority apps of the converged future. Cross-promotion between the pay-per-view and pay-free services is part of the Corporation's basic activities. A successful model, which used crosslinks among the primary Channel 4, E4 and the Internet, was Big Brother2. Another model of cross-media usage is educational production, where 4Learning appears competent in producing commercial and socially relevant contents. At the same time, it also responds to the government's request to use new technologies for educational purposes. 4Learning broadcasts school programme, and publishes books and videos, which it justifies as part of the Corporation's mission because school contents "cannot" occupy time space on the primary channel.

Technological development

New services mean keeping pace with technological developments, new media and platforms. Channel 4 orders technological developments from external software companies. Internet and interactive TV have proved very effective. The pay-per-view channel E4 is a "development lab" of Channel 4 devoted to innovation and risk projects that the primary channel cannot afford.

Proliferation

Proliferation of media services dictates a »portfolio« approach to the Corporation's activities and production. That requires all elements of the whole process to be checked in terms of synergy effects (economic, cultural and technological). Strategists emphasize the importance of economic and technological synergies among pay-per-view channels, Internet, interactive services and the primary channel. That could represent a hidden purpose of preparing the channels for a future when narrow TV channels intend to cover small market niches.

Channel 4 is a unique model of a public-commercial broadcaster in the UK and Europe. It combines two broadcasting models (public and commercial) in one corporation. The study of historical reasons for its creation and an analysis of its governance have made it possible to define its social context.

Within the context of the recession in advertising and other developments in the media remit, the business-oriented and diversity-oriented strategies were the right reaction. A positive corporate strategy was also to rejuvenate the audience by attracting young viewers (users) and encourage creativity of programmes. Innovation was demonstrated in applying state-of-the-art technologies and mixing different genres.

Channel 4 is a hybrid model of a mixed management system (commercial-public), which requires presentation of its environmental context.

Channel 4's environmental context

A media organization has to be studied within the contexts of its cultural, political and economic remit (Porter, 2003; Van Cuilenburg, 1998; McQuail, 2000). For this purpose, the McQuail's model was used (2000: 250).

Political-economic context of Channel 4

The actors of *economic-political pressures* are all stakeholders in the British media market: competitors, advertisers, owners and trade unions. All of them set political-economic frameworks for the performance of Channel 4. Competitors of Channel 4 are the public service BBC, the commercial stations ITV and Channel 5, as well as all cable and satellite channels. The state regulates the operation of Channel 4 and its competitors by setting and abolishing commitments under broadcasting licences, and by defining media acquisitions and interaction of transnational corporations through legislation. Trade unions also play an important role in the media remit. The state, which creates the national communications policy, significantly affects distribution channels in respect of technological developments and competition. Advertisers and economic circumstances put a particular pressure on Channel 4 as the sole broadcaster with the nation-wide permit for advertising, in contrast with other terrestrial rivals that hold broadcasting licences only for regional remits. The advertisers' impact appears in different forms that are often difficult to detect. Bogart (1995: 93–94) detects a huge impact by advertisers on media contents. Altschull (1984) draws attention to the content of news, which always expresses the interests of those who fund the programme.

Channel 4 was established as the fourth channel (precisely, as a third "national" television organization) in Britain because the economic situation allowed additional players into the media market. The decision on creating a new TV channel had the political aim of providing a rival to the BBC besides ITV. A sufficient financial potential in the market allowed it to earn its income solely by commercial activities. The decision to create Channel 4 came at the end of 1970s. Scarcity of frequency space dictated a political consensus about the decision, careful consideration of the usage of a broadcasting licence, and strict monitoring of the use of frequencies.

Channel 4 got political support. Nevertheless, it had to ensure financial independence from the socio-political system by earning all income in the advertising market. The funding formula provided a protective mechanism to safeguard the basic source of its livelihood. Economic conditions, however, enabled Channel 4 to keep on earning income from advertising without using the funding formula. Its independent activity in the advertising market brought even better financial results. The size of the advertising market was crucial for Channel 4.

The government's decision to finance new technologies and media services encouraged Channel 4 to start actively developing and investing in new programmes and pay-per-view services. That also ensured an additional source of income and a leading role in the overlapping of traditional and new media in the British media remit. The state's focus on the development and adoption of new technologies has supported the Corporation's further orientation towards innovation and earning of additional revenue.

Political-cultural context of Channel 4

Political-cultural pressures and their interrelationship determine the context in which a broadcasting organization shall perform. It has to commit to the regulatory framework imposing the fulfilment of a social mission, and to interests of pressure groups and other social institutions. In contrast with other industries, the political-cultural context of the media industry closely relates to the essence of its performance, which is the fulfilment of a particular social mission. Relations between the political and media systems are essential. The political system is closely tied with the media remit, its leadership and performance output (McQuail, 2000: 211). There are many reasons. The most important is legislation and regulation of media, which guarantees freedom of expression, and imposes particular commitments on media (especially public service). TV organizations reflect the political culture of its remits. The British media environment features a long tradition of public broadcasting service and a 50-year trend towards market-driven performance. Pressure groups that play an important role with regulatory authorities and various social initiatives co-create political culture, treating media performance not as one among other activities, but as a paramount social factor. Channel 4 promotes national culture, which it demonstrates by paying particular attention to the national film production. The political-cultural context also features the developments and culture of its remit. Channel 4's political support focuses on the programmes for and about minorities and ethnic groups. It pays heed to legislative and regulatory commitments and public opinion. Customers are an essential element within the political-cultural and political-economic context. Channel 4 observes their interests, demands and wishes by satisfying public interests as a public service, and by providing broadcast products and services as a business-oriented company.

The British Conservative government highlighted arguments for the increase of British production in electronic media and demonstrated that it supported British production by establishing Channel 4. BBC and ITV used mainly internal production capacities. That is why independent companies could hardly penetrate broadcasting corporations with their film and television production. Therefore, lobbying by independent production companies was a driving force in the campaign for the establishment of Channel 4. They argued that there existed a remit and a need for a new TV, which would support British production more than anyone else did. Channel 4 was also created to provide maximum support to independent production.

The political-cultural argument for creating the media policy of a new public broadcaster was a need to particularize social missions of all media organizations in the UK. That resulted in the detailed specification of commitments imposed on the new public broadcaster for the allocation of a broadcasting licence. The Channel 4's programme must provide a full range of contents that meet the needs of minority groups as specified in the decision on the allocation of the broadcasting licence. It is committed to educating and informing the public, and to promoting innovation and encouraging British independent production. The political-cultural argument for the creation of Channel 4 stemmed from the high potential of British independent production, which at that time could not stake out a place in the broadcasting industry.

In the context of British media policy, Channel 4 operates as one among several public broadcasters[50] that pursue the public mission. Channel 4 is obliged to provide particular programme contents to fulfil its social mission. It also has to take account of other TV's programmes and performance and cater for a complementary programme.

Channel 4 operates in a particular media remit featuring the political, cultural and social characteristics of British society. Freedom of the media, media pluralism, professionalism in journalism, the tradition of democracy in British society and the great importance paid to morally and socially acceptable activity make the British media broadcasting service unique compared to other environments. The importance of public opinion, the openness and accessibility to the public remit contributed to a Channel 4's unique media strategy. The specific political culture of British society helped make a light-touch media regulation efficient. A proposal for even looser monitoring of the media and the telecommunication industry is therefore on its way.

Language concerns, as one of the essential imperatives of media industry, are radically different in the British media remit compared to those in small countries. That is why smaller nations have to adopt a much more restrictive programme policy in respect of contents from the global market, in order to safeguard the cultural and national heritage of their languages.

Institutional context of Channel 4

Impacts, interests and the performance of leadership, media professionals, as well as technological potentials and limitations, determine the *institutional context of Channel 4*. The institutional context cannot remain outside the political-economic and political-cultural contexts, because their interrelations and interactions affect and determine the performance of the medium. The internal segmentation of the media organization into three dominant work cultures causes an inherent source of tension and divergence. Engwall (1978) focuses on the specific nature of work in a media organization and a source of conflicts arising from inherent relationships. Media organizations have to cope with the

50 Most European countries have only one public TV. The UK has many jointly exercising a particular public mission.

reconciling of interests among the three key segments: technology, media professionals (such as the creative force) and leadership. In addition, they have to track the rapidly developing technology and engage creative professionals to meet the public interest and achieve economic success. A rough segmentation of the broadcasting sector into the creative and pragmatic part is evident in management, which separates the production from the programming and broadcasting. Such an organizational structure reflects particular management approaches, which could quickly respond to environmental developments, and were needed to achieve the efficiency and effectiveness of an organization.

Channel 4's management structure follows a principle of a "non-traditional" broadcasting organization that produces and broadcasts programmes as a publisher. Most of its programming has to derive from external production companies. Such a non-traditional form of television is a very rational and efficient structure, which in addition creates an external market of creative and technological human resources.

Channel 4 is positioned as an exclusive and creative television, which it also expresses by its trademark. Its ambition was to play a complementary role and fill the gap in the media market that occurred between the public service BBC and commercial ITV. It creates its corporate culture as a television that caters for both minorities and the majority of society. Its strict programme criteria commit it to fulfil the minorities' needs, while its market-driven rationale allows it also to meet the majority interests.

The organization has constantly to reconcile conflicts between the business-oriented approach and the public service rationale to meet its social mission. However, conflicts between social responsibility and business rationale may produce synergy effects at all management levels and affect the organizational culture, which differs from the BBC's and ITV's.

The analysis of Channel 4 concentrates on the management of public-commercial service based on the criteria set for assessing the performance output and the efficiency of management approaches. Traditional criteria helped in examining how it met the public interest, while economic criteria provided evaluation as a market-oriented and a profit-oriented commercial organization. The purpose of the analysis was mainly to identify various management approaches that are necessary to meet the public interest and ensure economic success.

Examination of management strategies and practices, and observance of other public-service broadcasters in the national remit, provided a critical evaluation of the Channel 4's performance. The political-economic, political-cultural and institutional contexts of the Corporation were taken into account, because of cultural, political and economic factors that affect it at different levels.

Taking account of its environmental structure, the study of programming strategies and assessment of performance output provided an analytical outline of the Corporation and drew attention to the critical moments in its management. The study concentrates on the performance of Channel 4 within its remit and does not extend to the applicability of its model to other environments. That is due to the particular nature of British environment and the many factors that affected its positioning. The study deals with corporate management approaches and explores possibilities of their implementation in a public-commercial broadcasting service. The analysis of Channel 4 yielded theoretical guidelines for the functioning of the TV in the future. Forecasts for Channel 4 and the BBC diverge significantly. Projections for the BBC are tied to the government budgeting, while Channel 4 observes social and cultural values, universality and in particular, minority interests. Channel 4 favours financial stability, innovation and diversity in respect of demographic characteristics.

7. Applicability of Management Methods of a Hybrid Broadcasting Model

This chapter summarises the main research findings on broadcasting management. An analysis of the broadcasting model reveals that successful performance of a public service TV organization needs to meet two objectives: the mission of public good and economic efficiency. That is an imperative for survival in the dynamic liberalized media market. Both goals, as well as overall effectiveness, can be achieved if modern management approaches are adopted.

The research defines requirements for an increase of effectiveness and efficiency of broadcasting organizations, especially public services that must pursue a particular mission and meet economic efficiency at the same time. The study seeks and identifies more efficient management approaches and ways of developing methods for assessing effectiveness and efficiency.

The effectiveness of the broadcasting organization that serves as a case study is examined through indicators of economic efficiency and public interest. A public-commercial TV organization represents a hybrid broadcasting model that combines characteristics of the commercial and public service broadcasting industry.

We determined that it is possible effectively to reconcile public interest (with respect to political criteria) with economic interests in individual segments. In order for a public-commercial television organization to achieve these combined objectives, it was necessary to introduce modern management approaches. They comprise the development of assessment criteria for effectiveness and efficiency, flattening of the management structure, rational management of production resources, efficient content management, defining and examining target audiences, and implementation of innovations and new technologies at all levels. The essential feature of the management process is efficient content management, which takes account of the organization's objectives and defines programme production. The study also shows that the management process in the modern media environment concentrates on the programme contents and not on the TV channel. Today, viewers choose among the host of TV channels those contents they attract them and not a TV channel they are loyal to. Loyalty to the channels has become out of date.

The study demonstrated that economic efficiency and public interest could be successfully reconciled in a mixed commercial-public TV model subject to modern management approaches.

This book presents a study of a media organization's performance and its context. Furthermore, it highlights a particular nature of the media product and describes various management practices. The primary research method is a case study providing an understanding and explanation of the whole process. The case study of the Channel 4 model explores mixed management approaches that this unique public-commercial broadcasting organization uses to meet its public mission and economic interests at the same time. Due to its public-commercial nature, the Channel 4 hybrid model combines characteristics of public and commercial broadcasting systems. Channel 4 is a unique broadcasting model, which is comparable with other TV models only in individual elements. Such a complex case study provides an understanding not only of the organization itself but also of the historical circumstances, theoretical framework and current developments within its remit. In particular, the study concentrates on understanding Channel 4's management process aimed at reaching its institutional goals.

For the study of Channel 4's management practices and ways of achieving organizational objectives, a model for assessing performance output was designed to help explain performance results. The model for assessing performance output observes the peculiarity of a media organization that is required to fulfil the public interest and follow the free market rationale. The model for assessing performance output served as a framework for the study of the management process within the television institution. The study of a hybrid-broadcasting model can help one to learn how to reconcile and fulfil objectives of a media organization.

The model features several peculiarities that make it appropriate only for a particular social environment; it cannot be used as a whole in other media environments. Its applicability is based on modern management approaches that could contribute to the fulfilment of public and economic interests. Peculiarities of political-economic and political-cultural contexts, and the institutional position of the organization, are also highlighted as crucial. The existing model combining mixed management practices provides unique management approaches that ensure effective performance by the organization in its peculiar environment. Modern approaches that contribute to a better performance output in other social environments are efficient content management, examination of population groups and implementation of new technologies in traditional media.

The aim of the research was to study Channel 4 as a hybrid-broadcasting model and determine successful modern management approaches that help in realizing public and economic interests. An analysis of the creation, development, performance, advantages and disadvantages of Channel Four Television Organisation can contribute to the theory and practice of media management, particularly in broadcasting. It can enrich the theoretical foundations of the interdisciplinary science of communication policy, which also solves the dilemma how to satisfy public and profit-oriented interests.

The key thesis of this research project was to demonstrate that the strength of successful management lies in coordination of both goals: responsibility to the public and to the owners, in other words meeting both the public good and economic efficiency, which has been proven through the case study. The book derives from the hypothesis that providing economic efficiency and meeting the public good are not entirely separate categories. The particular social mission of a mass medium (television, both public and private) is to inform, educate and entertain, while observing and strengthening the values of the democratic, cultural and educational mission. Such a mission cannot be realized without performance effectiveness. That is why it is necessary to take account of the free market rationale and achieve economic efficiency, which ultimately can maintain social values as part of particular social mission. The purpose of television is to reach target publics, and to produce programmes that would attract a particular (or the broadest possible) audience, since television »sells its products« to viewers. If television does not succeed in »selling« its programmes to viewers, it fails to achieve commercial efficiency as well as its social mission. The viewers justify the existence of television.

Changes that affected media environment over the past decade have also changed the character of broadcasting. The broadcasting industry has to follow the market-oriented rationale. Its performance is embedded in a competitive environment occupied by domestic and foreign media players and driven by rapid technological and political changes. Changed conditions place additional demands on public television to increase earnings in the market and simultaneously justify its role and social mission. Television has to define a vision and a strategy how to succeed in meeting the mission within the context of rapid political and economic developments in society. New circumstances have modified the character of the PBS, which used to be decidedly non-commercially oriented. Perception of television as a non-commercial institution of high culture has lost its solid ground in today's changed social circumstances. In today's digital expansion involving diverse channels and programmes, public television is just one of the players in the market. Its role is far from being self-understood, because the mission alone does not justify its existence, and it is apparently not indispensable either. Market liberalisation requires stricter performance criteria for public service institutions. In today's market-driven society with a host of private players tracking economic rationale and the highest possible cost-efficiency, adoption of such a rationale by public service broadcasters is obviously necessary in modern social systems. Mixing of private and public managerial practices requires the setting of more appropriate standards for the functioning of a whole range of social services. Governance of public television has acquired in this way a larger scope and more demanding tasks, which include modern management approaches and achievement of the social mission and economic success.

The theoretical examination and analysis of the case study highlights the characteristics of a broadcasting model that successfully works in the UK. A hybrid-broadcasting model was successfully conceived and developed thanks to a favourable economic, cultural, political and institutional environment. The case study presents particular features of the political, economic, cultural and institutional contexts, which provided a suitable environment for the development of a hybrid-broadcasting model.

In Britain, television is not treated as a public broadcasting service but as a public broadcasting system including both public and private televisions, which together exercise a particular social mission. The state demands fulfilment of a particular social mission also by commercial broadcasters, while other countries leave this issue to free market forces. Setting high standards of social mission for all terrestrial broadcasters paves the way for a long-term development strategy for the entire media remit. The state exercises these demands and controls by means of legislation and regulatory bodies, and expectations are defined by agreement with all television institutions. Cooperation among regulatory bodies and media institutions enables easier tracking of the umbrella strategy that takes account of the market rationale and at the same time places social mission at the centre as the principal standard of all televisions.

The British media policy is unique among European countries in its cultural-political perspective of the public television system. An analysis of the social environment in Slovenia could be useful in examining the possibility of implementing a whole or part of the hybrid-broadcasting model. A thorough study of the social environment in Slovenia in its political-cultural, political-economic and institutional contexts could expose ways of using the successful management approaches of the hybrid-broadcasting model. We believe that certain of these management strategies and approaches would enrich the Slovenian cultural environment. They could help encourage creative human capacities and earn additional revenue for this public service broadcaster, which suffers from economic, performance and organizational inefficiency.

The majority of management approaches and strategies are subjected to a national vision concerning the development of a public broadcasting service that is governed in the national interest by the state. Pursuant to the national media strategy, the state has to make two fundamental decisions: to decide how to fund operations and invest in new technologies. All decisions have to observe the particular status of public television as an important social institution exercising a particular social mission and promoting economic development.

Useful approaches in media management

The purpose of this chapter is to highlight successful management approaches and strategies detected in the case study of the hybrid-broadcasting model. In order to achieve the combined objectives of the public-commercial broadcasting organization, it was necessary to observe modern management approaches. They comprise a flattening of the management structure, rational management of production resources, efficient content management, definition and examination of target audiences, and innovation and implementation of new technologies at all levels. We first present the criteria for performance output essential in assessing the effectiveness of a broadcaster.

- Development and assessment of effectiveness and efficiency by various criteria: For this purpose, a utility model was developed to study the performance output of a public-commercial broadcaster, taking into account political and economic criteria.
- Change in editorial policy: A fundamental change in editorial policy derives from the programming and the management process, which generates ideas for the contents by observing the needs and objectives of the entire organization. Modern management strategies require target publics to be defined first, with allocation of adequate airtime in the programming. On this basis, programmes for the needs of individual target groups are produced. Most public broadcasters, including RTV Slovenija, design programming after TV products (broadcasts) have already been made. Such an approach, which fails to manage contents at an early stage, results in inadequate market share, a blurred picture of target viewers for particular products and indistinct accountability on the part of the producer. The whole management process should focus on efficient content management, which becomes crucial already in the phase of an initial creative idea for a product. Content management is critical for reaching corporate goals, based on economic efficiency and public interest.
- Separation of broadcasting publishing from production: Programming is a publisher's and not a producer's tool. In order to achieve greater effect, publishing has to be isolated from programme production. The publisher decides on what kind of programme it needs with respect to the corporate strategy, economic efficiency and public interest, and the production unit realizes it. Organizing broadcasting as a publisher rather than a producer gives several advantages. External production units take responsibility for the products;

such an organization is more cost-effective because creative human resources are tied to the projects of production units and not to the publisher. RTV Slovenia combines the functions of publishing and production under one roof. That causes unclear responsibility for broadcast products, which require substantial material resources that cannot be justified by the needs of a single organization. The social mission could also be exercised more effectively if production were rationally organized in several market-oriented production units. That would encourage creativity and generate tremendous potential for creative production.

- Providing mixed programme genres: New trends in programming combining different genres in a single product (for minority or majority tastes) enable a broadcaster simultaneously to meet the goals of both the public and economic interest.
- Integrating non-commercial contents subject to different assessment criteria: It is important to create non-commercial contents that are subject to other assessment criteria than the purely commercial. They are important because they are indicators of the organization's reputation and the fulfilment of its social mission.
- Studying characteristics of target audiences: Seeking demographic and time gaps allows the selection and attraction of narrow target groups. A study of the demographic structure of the target audience[51] is an important management approach, because the broadcaster's mission is to provide contents for wide-range or/and narrow-range target groups, and thereby satisfy various social interests. Many European PBSs still do not focus on demographic and other attributes of target audiences or pay attention to the characteristics, trends, interests and needs of targeted publics. Such practice neglects the role of individuals and social groups and allows the public television to operate irrespective of social developments, not satisfying either public or economic interests. Such conduct leads PBSs away from social reality, causes performance and economic inefficiency, and paves the way for competitive media players.
- Taking advantage of earning revenue in the free market: In the case of budgetary funding (subscription, subventions), the organization's productivity is not transparent. That is why criteria of productivity and the all-important use of human and other resources cannot be used in the examination of performance

51 The survey emphasizes the importance of examining the demographic structure of target audiences. However, it does not explore the issue of segmentation based on demographic structures, which is an important aspect of the study of media management and the social mission.

output or the assessment of management efficiency. PBSs suffering from ineffectiveness of production resources and the workforce cannot use criteria of productivity. Therefore, performance output cannot be assessed precisely, and corporate development strategies cannot take into account critical indicators. An absence of permanent government subventions leads towards independence from politics and concentration on two core objectives: satisfying public interest and meeting economic efficiency. Guaranteed financial resources often curtail organizational flexibility causing delayed responses to social developments.
- Flattening of organizational structure: Organizational flexibility and empowering organizational units are crucial for the independence of corporate departments and units. The effectiveness of such an approach generates a rapid response to social changes and a more efficient performance of corporate departments, which accept accountability for own output.
- Introducing new technologies to traditional broadcasting: Dynamic management generates innovation, commercial competitiveness and an efficient corporate management structure. Introduction of new technologies into the traditional medium, and expansion of new services afford many advantages: strengthening of the corporate trademark, increase of market share, rejuvenation of the audience and efficient deployment of all human and production resources. An organization that facilitates and transfers innovation and creativity to the technological level encourages the linking of traditional and new media, the use of synergies by providing new services, and additional revenue earned by creative products.

In the study, attention was drawn to the peculiarities of British society hosting a hybrid-broadcasting model, which shows little scope for implementing the whole model in another social environment. However, it also shows that the management approaches and strategies presented could be useful for the Slovenian environment. They would improve the functioning of both public and commercial broadcasters and enrich the entire Slovenian media remit.

Applicability of a hybrid-broadcasting model to RTV Slovenia

The book deals with the issue of media management, particularly the management of a broadcasting institution that is assigned a particular position in society. A glance at dynamic social developments demonstrates the necessity for the broadcasting organization to adapt not only to the national but also to the global environment. Effectiveness of management is examined through various traditional and economic criteria. The study of the hybrid-broadcasting model has detected management approaches that make a media organization capable of achieving the set goals. Hence, management practices deriving from the hybrid-broadcasting model deserve all attention. These approaches are legitimate enough to be generalized and applied to other public broadcasting services such as RTV Slovenia.

The hypothesis of the study is that a media organization pursues three fundamental objectives in any environment:

- satisfying the public interest (political goal)
- achieving effectiveness and efficiency (economic goal)
- making commitments to technology and utilizing converging technologies within the medium(technological goal)

Public broadcasting service RTV Slovenia

Slovenia has a rich history of radio and television broadcasting. Pilot transmissions of radio, which is now part of RTV Slovenija, started in Ljubljana on 1 September 1928. Radio was an extremely powerful means of propaganda like everywhere else in the world. In 1949, the first broadcasting laboratory started working in Ljubljana and launched trial TV broadcasts. In October 1958, RTV Ljubljana commenced regular broadcasting. RTV Ljubljana, a predecessor of RTV Slovenia, was part of the Yugoslav broadcasting system (JRT). The independent Republic of Slovenia established RTV Slovenija in 1992. It is the sole Slovenian public service, broadcasting on three TV channels.

RTV Slovenija is a public, non-profit broadcasting organization that carries out radio and television broadcasting, and other activities in compliance with statutory provisions. RTV Slovenija is subject to the Media Act (2006) and the Radiotelevizija Slovenija Act (2005). Its initiator is the National Assembly of the Republic of Slovenia. In accordance with the Radiotelevizija Slovenija Act, the public institution RTV Slovenija commits to producing two national TV programmes and three national radio programmes. In addition, it has to broadcast one TV and one radio programme for each of the Italian and the Hungarian minority groups. Furthermore, it must produce radio and TV programmes for Slovenian minority groups in neighbouring countries, and radio and TV programmes for the regional broadcasting centres RTV Koper and RTV Maribor. All the programmes have to be of high quality and diverse, providing informative, cultural, and educational and entertainment contents. RTV Slovenija must also create, reproduce and transmit cultural works of art, as well as shows for Slovenian ethnic groups, expatriates and guest workers across the world. RTV Slovenija also produces radio and television shows for the Roma ethnic community. In addition, it provides the national channel TV SLO 3 with live broadcasts and recordings of sessions of the Slovenian National Assembly and its working bodies.

National programmes have to reach at least 90 percent of the population of the Republic of Slovenia. The contents for Italian and Hungarian minority groups must cover 90 percent of the territory inhabited by these ethnic groups [Uradni list RS (Official Gazette of the Republic of Slovenia)].

The public institution RTV Slovenia is funded by multiple sources: licence fee, commercial revenue, marketing activity, government budget, sponsorship and other sources pursuant to the law and the statute. Subject to payment of the licence fee are holders of radio and TV receivers in those parts of the territory of the Republic of Slovenia where technical conditions enable reception of at least one channel of RTV Slovenija. The number of licence fee payers exceeds 600,000 (RTV Slovenija Annual Report, 2011–2013.) and the share of income from public funding is increasing (Table: Structure of total revenue realized in 2010–2013).

TV Slovenija provides various programme contents within individual genres. The *news programme* consists of daily and weekly news, current affairs and journals. The *culture and arts programme* consists of eight editorial programme units (education, film and series, culture and arts, children and youth, foreign films, documentaries, music and ballet, religion). The *entertainment programme* includes a variety of weekly shows and individual projects. The *sports programme* comprises a variety of broadcasts and sport events.

RTV Slovenija launched the MMC multimedia centre at the end of 2001, following the EBU directive on the introduction of multimedia services into broadcasting services. MMC's principal tasks are the development of multimedia applications, interactive support to radio and television programmes, and keeping in touch with multimedia developments. In addition, MMC incorporates editorial boards for teletext, web and mobile portals, subtitling for the deaf and partially deaf and an audio/video archive (AVA). Since 2004, MMC manages Info Channel, which also consists of two children's portals.

In December 2010, RTV Slovenija discontinued transmissions of its analogue signal and six months later completely converted to digital broadcasting. Programmes are provided through various platforms:

- terrestrial WLANs across Slovenia
- IPTV networks across Slovenia
- Cable networks across Slovenia and contractual countries for re-emitting.
- satellite transmissions
- Internet
- mobile devices

In 1995, the publisher Pro Plus launched the commercial channel POP TV and later also took over the commercial channel Kanal A. RTV Slovenija is the largest production and programming organization in Slovenia. Its activities are partially funded by public resources, and a large part of revenue also comes from advertising. RTV Slovenija, like other PBSs in Europe, needs to increase its share of commercial income, and this dictates the implementation of modern management methods to enhance cost-efficiency.

Modern management approaches for RTV Slovenija

Loss of market share, the search for a new corporate identity as the public service broadcaster, and delays in responding to harsh market conditions pose a serious threat to the legitimacy of RTV Slovenija. Management and efficiency of media organization are subjected to social conditions. Hence, management approaches of the hybrid-broadcasting model are explained in the context of RTV Slovenija.

Development and assessment of effectiveness and efficiency by various criteria

Using criteria for performance output is essential to assess the broadcaster's effectiveness. Besides traditional (political) measures imposed by law, a range of economic criteria is proposed:

- *Providing the public with efficient utilization of resources available*
- *Maximizing ratings of individual audiences*
  - examining average daily ratings
  - examining average programme ratings
- *Maximizing external resources*
  - maximizing advertising revenue
  - maximizing sales of programmes
- *Maximizing efficiency*
  - making efficient utilization of resources
  - providing reserves to production

The model proposed for assessing the efficiency of RTV Slovenija could contribute to the programming efficiency of all TV channels. The supervisory board of RTV Slovenija observes political criteria imposed by law, which however fail to thoroughly assess the organization's effectiveness. Hence, the hypothesis is posited that the use of economic criteria (maximization of audience, external resources, efficiency) could clearly indicate the organization's efficiency and contribute to the long-term legitimacy of RTV Slovenija.

Change in editorial policy

Programming management requires that relevant contents should be sought and provided for individual target groups subject to the content and time priorities of the target group. RTV Slovenija, employing the largest production and human resource capacity, often decides on producing new media products relevant to the capacities available rather than the needs of potential target audiences. A changed editorial policy could result in programming that would generate products for targeted audiences, scheduled with concern for their preferred airtime. After all, the programming potential is not realized until it reaches the target audience in the appropriate way and time. Programming management is crucial in prioritizing of contents, because it substantially contributes to the achievement of targeted and needed market shares.

Separation of broadcasting publishing from production

Practices with separate publishing and production activities yield higher cost-efficiency because of clear accountability for each media unit. The weakness of such an approach is in the ignoring of potential creative forces. On the other hand, it excels in rational exploitation of production capacities. The current organizational structure of RTV Slovenija blurs accountability among the procurement units, production units, and programming and broadcasting units. Separation of publishing activity from production brings advantages by making the organization efficient. In the final analysis, launching a new media product has to stem from the need to attract a particular target audience and satisfy a particular population group. A TV institution has to order such a product and test it in pilot production in order to reach a targeted audience.

The publisher can thus reduce the risk of a product turning out inappropriate, and set precise parameters for the production of a new product. Such an approach could bring RTV Slovenija higher efficiency and improve the quality of most of its entertainment contents. It would also encourage creative capacities in the media environment and strengthen the social mission of public television.

Providing mixed programme genres

The trend towards mixing programming genres becomes popular also on RTV Slovenija, bringing higher ratings of different publics and better long-term yield. Mixing educational and entertainment genres, and informative and entertainment contents, could contribute to a more efficient realization of traditional political objectives too.

Integrating non-commercial contents subject to different effectiveness criteria
Education and news are subject to a maximum extent to non-economic criteria. News on a public broadcasting service sets the character of the entire institution, helping it to establish an identity that distinguishes it from commercial media.

Studying characteristics of target audiences

Knowing the characteristics of population groups as media audiences is essential for corporate efficiency. RTV Slovenia aims to reach the widest possible audiences during airtime. That requires a profound knowledge of population groups with respect to preferences and the time space they would devote to television.

Creating advantage by earning revenue in the free market

Various kinds of funding sources can reduce risks of insufficient income, which happens in a sole-source funding formula. Funding by licence fees is quite safe in terms of economic fluctuations, but it can be risky in terms of the dependence upon current political decisions. Such a guaranteed source of funding often contributes to smaller ratings too. Earning a larger share of income in the free market requires paying more attention to the preferences of individual target audiences and design of more flexible programming.

Flattening of organizational structure

Efficient management that enhances the dynamic performance of individual departments is crucial for corporate effectiveness. Empowered departments produce added value. Autonomous departments also take a large part of responsibility for decision-making and therefore strive for efficient performance of their units, and consequently of the entire organization. Only relative autonomy of organizational units and a flat management structure ensure quick response to market developments. Such an approach could help RTV Slovenija to increase efficiency and effectiveness.

Introducing new technologies to traditional broadcasting

Technological innovations are the driving force for media development. It would be reasonable also for RTV Slovenija to follow the practice of Channel 4, which has been testing new approaches and launching new services since its foundation. A public broadcasting organization can also play a significant role in the market by vigorous implementation of technological innovations and providing quality up-to-date contents.

Implementation of the proposed model is advocated in the light of the study of the organization's effectiveness and its requirement to observe political and economic goals. The proposed management method is found to be to a large extent appropriate for RTV Slovenija. Modern approaches generate efficient content management, profound knowledge of population groups, a clear separation of publishing from production activities, and introduction of new technologies into traditional media. Thereby they contribute to a better performance output of media in different social environments. Modern management approaches also support the fulfilment of public interest and the broader social mission that public broadcasting services are committed to.

The context of RTV Slovenija presented provides a more explicit evaluation of the organization's position.

Context of the public service RTV Slovenija

Political-economic context

RTV Slovenija has been the sole public (formerly national) broadcasting service since its foundation. The market size allows a limited number of media players, because the volume of advertising revenue is much smaller than in larger European countries. Consequently, reasonable chances for the survival of a large number of broadcasters are small. The economic situation of RTV Slovenija could not support being funded solely from advertising revenue. Commercial broadcasters are also strong rivals for advertising. The licence fee, which is the principal source of funding today, and is expected to be also in the future, needs political support in terms of its size. Therefore, debates on the licence fee always acquire political dimensions, because political support also means covering the needs of current political elites. Trends towards political independence are obvious; however, the link with current political decision-makers is still indispensable because it facilitates stable funding through the licence fee. Particularities of the Slovenian political-economic context affect both the management structure and the programme contents of the public broadcasting service.

Political-cultural context

The need for a public broadcasting service in Slovenia is also demonstrated by the promotion and maintenance of national identity. We present an outline of principal guidelines that the public broadcasting service observes. Goals that can by fulfilled only by a media organization that receives public funds are obvious. They are to protect vulnerable social groups and preserve the language and cultural heritage of national importance. Providing contents without commercial connotation gives legitimacy for the usage of public funding. Linguistic obstacles in Slovenia are more complex than those, which larger nations face. That poses challenges and restrictions on programming too. RTV Slovenia represents the principal cultural institution in the national environment. The political-cultural context is particular also in the openness of media market, professional standards of the creative industry, and the absence of self-regulation compared to the British market.

Institutional context

RTV Slovenia faces apparent friction between a commercially oriented rationale tracking greater ratings and advertising revenue share on one hand and satisfying the public good and the interests of different social groups on the other hand. Such conflicts generate diversity in programming, but often also tensions within the organization as the result of different criteria for evaluating the organization's effectiveness. The corporate culture of RTV Slovenija mirrors the situation of most public broadcasting services in Europe. It is structured hierarchically and bureaucratically. Unlike Channel 4, RTV Slovenija is a producer and a publisher combined under one roof. However, the implementation of modern management approaches could enhance the efficiency of RTV Slovenija despite different corporate cultures; on the one hand tracking the broadest social interest and on the other searching for social gaps.

8. Conclusion

The results of the survey on electronic media, management of media organizations, and particularly the results of the case study, evidence interaction of various social disciplines and the extraordinary power of electronic media in today's world. Reconciling public and economic interests is the primary management task in media organizations nowadays. The case study of a hybrid media model draws attention to particular successful practices that could usefully serve in different social environments. Fast response to technological, political and economic change can undoubtedly help to achieve the primary goal of today's media – fulfilling the public interest and providing cost-effective products. Moreover, fulfilling public and economic interests requires efficient management of programme contents, which ensures the realization of a particular social mission and successful competitiveness in the market. Selection of target audiences and careful demographic studies are crucial for economic efficiency. In addition, the study reveals that independent market-driven financing (without government subventions) can be an advantage, because it requires efficient programme planning and constant control. Introducing new technologies into a TV operation is essential. Various new platforms attract the public, which strengthens the particular social and economic mission of broadcasting.

TV Slovenia is a public-service broadcaster. With its location in Central Europe, it is a significant partner to other public television services in the region. At the same time, it can serve as an important model for the transformation, which all public television stations should undergo. The case study of a hybrid media organization brings significant findings, which could help enhance the restructuring of public television stations. This study using political and economic criteria has succeeded in bringing out particular management approaches, which were identified as essential for successful performance of media organizations.

This book consists of the proposed theoretical assumptions, studies, empirical research, and of course the author's own observations of production processes. It aims at a better understanding of the role of media today. In particular, it aspires to contribute to responsible management of the power and impact of media as co-creators of social development.

Summary

The changed media environment in the last decade has caused changes in the performance of media, since they had to cope with technological, economic and political forces. The television broadcasting industry governed by a market-oriented rationale is heavily influenced by rapidly changing technology, economy and politics, as well as media rivals emerging from within and outside national borders. Overlapping between media industries, mergers and acquisitions, removal of legal barriers, the growth of strategic alliances and partnerships among media companies, as well as developments in the global entertainment media market and information, have dictated changes in media management. Media management has become very complex, since TVs have to reconcile various requirements imposed by the public, the owners, advertisers and society. In addition to various interests, they must take account of technological development, changes of regulatory policy and social trends.

Mixing of private and public managerial practices requires the setting of appropriate standards for the functioning of a vast range of social services. The right answer to the challenges that the TV institutions face is to be found in new management approaches: how to produce more with less resources in a heavily competitive market. The most essential demand imposed on the management of television institutions over the recent period is cost-efficient performance, involving not only economic efficiency but also operational and organizational efficiency. This demand is due to the new competitive environment in which public TVs operate. Most public institutions in all countries face such challenges for increased efficiency and flexibility. These challenges derive in particular from the growing complexity of society and interactions of various factors. They are also due to the need for quick responses to societal changes and integration with the global and information village. All of that requires a better coordination and greater participation in a period of increasing decentralization and scarcity of resources. Demands to reduce expenditure dictate effective approaches to management, administration and operations. They also demand development of systems for monitoring work processes and assessing performance output.

This book describes the issue of success and efficiency of public television, as well as the conflict of interests between a special social mission and economic efficiency. The starting point is an assumption that providing economic efficiency and meeting the public good can go hand in hand. Furthermore, the book offers a model for assessing the performance output of public-commercial television, based on political and economic criteria. A set of criteria used to explore the performance output of television organizations makes it possible to explain the significance of being actively engaged in the marketplace, which does not exclude fulfilling the public interest. This book proposes modern management practices for the successful performance of public TVs. In addition, it determines the management practices that could be applied to a public TV to achieve success.

The book presents the role of mass media in relation to the social environment in which they operate. Various theoretical hypotheses demonstrate the exclusive position of media, media economics and the uniqueness of media industry. The study of media organizations illustrates the public interest in all media and complexity of media policies.

The book exposes different approaches in management theories, and indicates their limitations in application to the media industry. The theoretical framework for the analysis of media management especially that of public television, consists of those theoretical approaches that contribute to quality analysis. Exploration of public TV management involves the fields of political science and administration, while economics and communication disciplines have helped in seeking appropriate models for achieving corporate goals.

The study of various TV systems reveals their status and challenges, and the obstacles they confront in their media markets. Characteristics of the US and European media systems are described. Much attention is paid to the dual TV broadcasting system in Europe, where public TVs have to compete with commercial players, while subjected to both a strict regulatory policy and free-market rationale. The UK television system and the hybrid-broadcasting model of Channel 4, together with the circumstances that paved the way to its foundation, serve as a case study.

Criteria for the study of the management and performance output of public television are also defined. These criteria make it possible to analyse the managerial process of a TV organization, and to show its strengths and weaknesses. The book also expounds the reasons for observing economic criteria as important indicators of successful management of public television, showing the degree of the organization's adjustment to the dynamic media environment.

The analysis of the management of a hybrid TV model can serve as a case study for public television organizations to assess their performance output and to evaluate their management practices. It also elaborates up-to-date management approaches that could be applied from the hybrid model to the public TV service. RTV Slovenia is identified as a public-service organization that could have recorded better results and enhanced its legitimacy if it had changed its management practices and assessment methods. The importance of the context in which individual media organizations operate is also elaborated. Each organization, especially a public service media institution, can enhance its legitimacy in society by organizational efficiency and performance success.

The book presents the main criteria for evaluating management approaches and performance assessment. With those criteria, it is possible to analyse the management process of broadcasting organizations and expose their strengths and weaknesses. Particular attention is also devoted to explaining the reasons for considering economic criteria in addition to political criteria. The economic parameters are necessary elements in the process of evaluating the management of public broadcasting. This shows us the level of accommodation of the broadcasting organizations to dynamic media environment.

The analysis of management of the hybrid-broadcasting model is devoted to the case study of the commercial public broadcaster Channel 4, which analyses its performance and management approaches. The hybrid media model can serve to determine modern management methods that can be applied to other media organizations, in this case to RTV Slovenia. The book presented the circumstances that contributed toward the success of hybrid broadcasting model, therefore the circumstances of broadcasting model were presented. The managerial criteria in broadcasting organisation also in Slovenia can be helpful tool toward success of broadcasting organisation in any country. Public service broadcasting all over the Europe in the last decade is calling for new approaches which are presented in the book.

Enclosures

Enclosure No. 1

Milestones of Channel Four Television Corporation:

1936 – BBC begins broadcasting from Alexandra Palace.

1955 – ITV London begins broadcasting as the first commercial television.

1969 – BBC and ITV start using the UHF 625-line system. Introduction of a fourth channel is technically feasible.

1971 – Independent Television Companies' Association asks for control over the fourth channel.

1979 – Conservative government grants control over the fourth channel to IBA.

1979 – Jeremy Isaacs, Chief Executive of Channel 4, announces in his historic speech that the programme should be for everyone at a time and not all the time for all. Their target is 10-percent viewing share.

1979 – ITC publishes a plan for the fourth channel as a non-profit publisher that would not produce its own programming, but buy and broadcast it.

1980 – Broadcasting Act comes into force.

1981 – Channel Four Television Corporation comes into operation.

1982 – Channel 4 starts broadcasting and reaches more than 87 percent of the British population.

1986 – A new leadership with Chief Executive Michael Grade is appointed, and adopts a more commercially-oriented editorial policy with stronger influence of American production.

1990 – Broadcasting Act is passed obliging Channel 4 to start selling its own advertising airtime pursuant to the funding formula agreed between ITV and Channel 4 (half of all Channel 4's revenues exceeding the 14-percent market share to be assigned to ITV, and 25 percent to the reserve fund of Channel 4).

1993 – Channel Four Television Corporation reaches a record of 12-percent viewing share.

1993 – Channel 4 is granted a renewed frequency licence imposing special responsibilities and obligations. Channel 4 starts selling its own advertising space.

1994 – Channel 4 reaches 38-percent viewing share in prime time and beats BBC and ITV for the first time.

1997 – A new commercial television, Channel 5, is launched.

1997 – A new leadership with managing director Michael Jackson is appointed; it follows the programming strategy of the previous management.

1998 – The funding formula agreed between Channel 4 and ITV is abolished. Channel 4 starts independent activities in the advertising market assuming sol responsibility for its budget.

1998 – ITC monitors and renews Channel 4's frequency license.

1998 – Channel 4 starts broadcasting the first pay-per-view programmes.

2001 – Appointment of a new leadership of Channel 4 with Chief Executive Mark Thompson.

Enclosure No. 2

A summary of the most relevant programming and institutional obligations of Channel 4, which ITC regularly monitored

Programme obligations: Ensuing from the Broadcasting Act, which prescribes that Channel 4 differentiate its identity from ITV, and provide the contents for those target groups whom ITV does not pay enough attention. In short, it serves particular tastes and not a standard taste.

The mission of Channel 4: The programme of Channel 4 is not expected to serve the general public. However, it shall target the highest possible ratings. Achieving a different character requires a different editorial choice in comparison to what other programmes deliver. Channel 4 has to hit all age groups and include coverage of international and global affairs.

Schools' programme: Channel 4 shall broadcast 330 hours a year for schools.

Educational contents: Channel 4 shall devote an average of seven hours a week to educational contents.

News and current affairs:* Channel 4 shall devote sufficient space to news and current affairs, which should be of high quality.

Religious programme: Programming must contain religious programmes in prime time and one hour a week at other times.

Multicultural programme: Since 1999, there must be at least three hours per week devoted to multicultural contents.

Investments in film: Channel 4 shall play the main role in the British film industry.

Special needs: Programmes shall be designed for people with disabilities.

European production: Most of the Channel 4's airtime shall be devoted to contents of European origin.

Independent production: Channel 4's programming shall contain 25 percent of programmes coming from independent production companies.

Originated production: Originated production is expected to occupy 60 percent of broadcast hours in prime time.

Repeats: Since 1999, repeats must occupy less than 40 percent of all broadcast hours, and no more than 20 percent in prime time.

Production outside London: 30 percent of the programme broadcast by Channel 4 shall be produced outside London.

Education: At least 0.5 percent of Channel 4's whole income shall be allocated to education.

Funding: Channel 4 has committed itself to financially support British film and programme production, and follow digital developments by investing in various platforms and new services.

Literature

Albarran, Alan B. (1998): The coalescence of power: transformation of the communications industries. V: R. G. Picard (ur.), *Evolving media markets: Effect of economic and policy changes* (p.p. 8–24). Turku: Economic Research Foundation for Mass Communication.

Albarran, Alan B. (2002): *Management of Electronic Media (2nd ed.).* North Texas: Wadsworth Thomson Learning.

Albarran, Alan B. in Chan-Olmsted, Sylvia (1998): *Global Media economics: Commercialization, and integration of world media markets.* Ames: Iowa State University Press.

Alexander, Alison, Owers, James in Carveth, Rod (1993): *Media economics: theory and practice.* Mahwah: Lawrence Erlbaum Associates, Inc.

Annex to the Review of the Future Funding of the BBC 1999, str. 202–203. London: BBC.

Atkinson, Dave in Raboy, Marc (eds) (1997): *Public Service broadcasting: the Challenges of the Twenty-firts Century.* Paris: UNESCO.

Bašić Hrvatin, Sandra. (2002): *Državni ali javni servis: perspektive javne radiotelevizije v Sloveniji.* Ljubljana: Mirovni inštitut.

BBC (1984–2002). Annual reports. www.bbc.co.uk

Blanchard, Simon in Morley, David, Morley (1982) *What's this Channel Four?* London: Comedia.

Block, Peter (ed.) (2001): *Managing in the Media.* Oxford: Focal Press.

Blumler, Jay G. (1992): *Television and the Public Interest: Vulnerable Values in West European Broadcasting.* London: Sage.

Blumler, Jay G. in Gurevitch, Michael (1982): The Political Effects of Mass Communication in the Media. V: *Culture, society and the Media* (Gurevitch, Michael ur.). London: Routledge.

Blumler, Jay G. in Gurevitch, Michael (1995): *The Crisis of Public Communication.* London: Routledge.

Born, Georgina (2002): *Strategy, Positioning and projection in Digital Television.* London: Sage.

Born, Georgina (2002): *Uncertain Future: Public Service Television and the Transition to Digital.* London: ESRC Final Award Report.

Bouckaert, Boudjewin (1994): "*Free Society*". Referat na seminarju »Svoboda in družba«, ki ga je pripravil Inštitut za humanistične študije na George Mason University. Julij 1994. San Francisco: College of Notre Dame.

Bourdieu, Pierre (1991): *Language and Symbolic Power*. Cambridge: Polity Press.

Boynton, G. R. (1996): Our Converations about Governing. V: *Political Communication Research* (ur. David Palez). Norwood, N. J.: Ablex Publishing.

Budd, Mike, Craig, Steve, Steinman, Clay (1999): "*Consuming Environments*". New Jersey: Rutgers University Press.

Cantor, Muriel (1985): *United States: A System of Minimal Regulation*. London-Sydney: Croom Helm.

Cantor, Murriel (1992): *Prime-time television*. Newbury Park: Sage.

Carles Llorens-Maluquer (2002): "*The European Union Policy, Pluralism and Public service Broadcasting*" Januar. Helsinki: RIPE.

Channel 4 Television Company (1995–2002): Statements and Promises. www.channel4.co.uk

Channel 4 Television Company Ltd (1994): *An Introduction and Guide for Producers*. London: Channel 4.

Channel 4 Televison Company Ltd (1984, 1985, 1986, 1987, 1988, 1989, 1990, 1991, 1992, 1993, 1994, 1995, 1996, 1997, 1998, 1999, 2000, 2001, 2002): *Report and Financial Statements*. London: Channel 4

Christians, Clifford G., Rotzoll, Kim B. in Fackler, Mark (1997): *Media ethics: cases and moral reasoning* (5th ed). New York: Longman.

Coleman, Howard (1982): *Case Studies in Broadcast Management: Radio and Television*. New York: Hasting House Publishers.

Collins, Richard (1988): *The economics of television*. London: Sage.

Collins, Richard in Murroni, Cristina (1996): "*New media new policies*". Cambridge: Polity Press.

Collins, Richard in Purnell, James (1996): The Future of BBC. in: *Javnost*, 3(2), 71–80. Ljubljana: EURICOM.

Corcoran, Francis (1996): 'Arts Council of te air: switching attention from the service to the programme'. V: *Javnost/Public*, 3 (2), str. 9–23. Ljubljana: EURICOM.

Corcoran, Paul E. (1979): *Political Language and Rhetoric*. Austin: University of Texas Press.

Corporation for Public Broadcasting Annual Report, 1997. Washington: Corporation for public Broadcasting.

Croteau, David, Hoynes, William (2001): *The Business of Media; Corporate Media and the Public Interest. Pine Forge Press.* California-London-New Delhi: Thousands Oaks.

Curran, James (1990): *Mass Media and Democracy.* Cambridge: Edward Arnold.

Dahlgren, Peter in Sparks, Colin (1991): *Communications and Citizenship.* London: Routledge.

Dahlgren, Peter, (1995): *Televison and the Public Sphere.* London: Sage.

Davis, James (1991): TV, *UK Special Report.* London: Knowledge Research.

Day, Louis A. (2000): *Ethics in media communications: Cases and controversies* (3rd ed.). Belmont: Wadsworth.

De Sola Pool, Ithiel (1990): *Technologies Without Boundaries.* Cambridge: Harvard University Press.

Deacon, David, Pickering, Michael, Golding, Peter, Murdock Graham (1999): *Researching Communications. A Practical Guide to Methods in Media and Cultural Analysis.* London: Arnold.

Department for Culture Media and Sport, Broadcsting Policy Devision, Digital Decisions: Viewer Choise and Digital Television. *A Report by the Viewers' Panel to the Secretary of State for Culture, Media and Sport.* (december 2001), para. 3.3. London.

Dignam, Colin (2002): Television's fuzzy future. In: *Broadcast*, 22. 11. 2002, 14–15. London: Broadcast Publisher.

Dimitras, Panayote E. (1997): 'Greece', 98–109. In: Bernt Stubbe Řstergard (ed.): *The media in Western Europe. The Euromedia Handbook.* London: Sage.

Docherty, David, Morrison, David E., Tracey, Michael (1988): *Keeping faith?* London: Libbey.

Dodd, Philip in Stevenson, Wilfried (2001): Creative industries and »joined-up« culture. In: S. Higdon (ed.): *Culture and Communications: perspectives on Broadcasting and the information Society.* London: Independent Television Commission, str. 128–133.

Licence requirements for Channel 4(1993, 1998). London: Ministry for culture, sport and education. UK.

Drucker, Peter F. (1999): *Management challenges of the 21st centrury.* New York: Harper Collins.

Drucker, Peter F. (2000, January 1): Interview. *The Wall Street Journal,* p. R34. New York.

Dunnett, Peter J. S. (1990): *The world television industry*. London: Routledge.

Dyson, Kenneth in Humphreys, Peter (ur.) (1990): *The political Economy of Communications: International and European Dimensions.* London-New York: Routledge.

Dyson, Kenneth H. F. (2000): *Broadcasting and new media policies in Western Europe*. London: Routledge.

Dyson, Kenneth in Humpreys, Peter (1988): *The Context of New Media Politics in Western Europe. Broadcasting and New Media Policies in Western Europe.* London: Routledge.

Eckhart, Richard (1994): Capital expenditure budgeting and controls. In: A. Gordon (ed.): *Understanding broadcast and cable finance* (str. 102–108). Atlanta: BCFM Press.

Engwall, Lars (1978): *Newspaper as Organizations*. Farnborough: Saxon House.

European Avdiovisual Observatory (1999). Strasbourg.

European Commission (1998): *The digital age: European Avdiovisual Policy.* Report from the high level group on avdiovisual Policy.

European Commission (2000): *Communication on Services of general interest in Europe*. COM (2000) 580 final.

European Commission (2001): *Communication from the Commission on the application of State aid rules to public service Broadcasting.*

Ferfila, Bogomil (1993): Od političnega menedžmenta do analize Evropske skupnosti in ZDA: široka pahljača podiplomskega študija politologije. V: *Delo*, let. 35, št. 250, 14.

Ferfila, Bogomil (1994): *Teme iz vladne ekonomske in vladnih politik*. Ljubljana: Enotnost.

Ferfila, Bogomil (2002): Mediji in politika v ZDA. In: *Teorija in praksa*, letn. 37, 5, p. 903–924. Ljubljana: FDV.

Folkerts, Jean in Teeter, Dwight C. (1989): *Voices of Nation: A History of the Media in the U. S.* New York: Macmillan.

Forester, Ted (ed.) (1985): *The Information Technology revolution*. Oxford: Basil Blackwell.

Galik, Mihaly in Denes, Ferenc (1993): "*From Command Media to Media Market: The Role of Foreign Capital in the Transition of the Hungarian Media*". Seminar at Budapest University of Economics (Department of Business Economics). July 1993, Budimpest.

Geiser, R. (2000): Management control in German television: Delivering numbers for management decisions. V: *The Journal of Media Economics*, 13 (2), 123–142. Mahwah: Lawrence Erlbaum Associates.

Gerbner, George (1964): "Institutional pressures on mass communicators". V: P. Halmos (ed.): *The Sociology of Mass Media Communicators*, str. 205–48.

Gitlin, Todd (1980): *The Whole World is Watching*. Berkeley: University of California Press.

Goodwin, Eugene (1983): *Media Ethics: Cases and Moral Reasoning*. New York: Longman.

Goodwin, Peter (1998): *Television under the Tories*. London: British Film Institute.

Goodwin, Peter (1999): *The television policies of the UK administrations of Margaret Thatcher and John Major 1979–1997*. London: British Film Institute.

Grade, Michael (1999): *It Seemed Like a Good Idea at the Time*. London: Macmillan.

Gurevitch, Michael (1994): "*Media and Mass Democracies: The Crisis of Communication for Citizenship*." Paper at the conference ELTE. June,1994, Budapest.

Haraszti, Miklos (1994): *"Free Media?"* Referat na Central European University (Lecture at department of political sciences, CEU, Budapest) May, 1994..

Harvey, Syliva (2000): Channel 4 Television: From Annan to Grade v British Television. A Reader. Ed. Edward Buscombe. Oxford: Clarendon Press.

Hasselbach, Suzanne (1992): *The regulation of the broadcasting infrastructure in Germany*. Knjiga: University Westminster, London, UK.

Held, Virginia (1970): *The Public Interest and Individual Interest*. New York: Basic Books.

Hoggart, Roger (1976): *Bad News*. Glasgow University Media Group. London: Routledge and Kegan Paul.

Hood, Stuart and Tabary-Petersen, Thalia (1997): *Broadcasting in Britain*. London: Pluto Press.

Hosmer, Larue T. (1991): *The ethics of management* (2nd ed.). Boston: Irwin.

Howe, Peter (1991): The 90's employee. V: *Broadcast Cable Financial Journal*, 5–6.

Hoynes, William (1994): *Public television for sale.* Boulder-Oxford: Westview Press.

Hujanene, Taisto. (2002): "*The Power of Schedule*". Tampere: Tampere University Press.

Independent Television Commission (1984, 1985, 1986, 1987, 1988, 1989, 1990, 1990, 1991, 1992, 1993, 1994, 1995, 1996, 1997, 1998, 1999, 2000, 2001, 2002) Annual Reports. London: ITC.

Iosifides, Petros (1996): *Media concentration policy in the European Union and the public interest.* London: University of Westminster.

Isaacs, Jeremy (1989): *Storm over 4*. London: Weidenfeld and Nicolson.

Ishikawa, Sakae and Muramatsu Yoko (1991): *Quality Assessment of Broadcasting Programming*. Studies of Broadcasting 27, str. 207–220.

ITC (1993) *Qualifying Revenue: Statement of Principles and Administrative Arrangements under the Broadcasting Act 1990.* London: ITC.

ITC (1996) *Channel 4 licence*. London: ITC.

ITC (1998) *Channel 4 licence*. London: ITC.

Jaska, James A. and Pritchard, Michael S. (1994): *Communication ethics*: U.S. v. NAB. IN: *Journal of Mass Media Ethics*, 4 (2), str. 214–231.

Johannesen, Richard L. (1987): *Ethics in Human Communication*, 2nd ed. Prospect Heights: Waveland.

Johanson, Cindy, lecture at the conference (March, 4–5, 2002): The public broadcaster and the digital future; Conference: New Media and Broadcasting. London: Financial Times.

Jones, Carwyn (1994): *Channel 4*. Journal of Press-Politics 1(2), str. 1–29.

Karen Siune in Olof Hulten, (1998): Does Public Broadcasting Have a Future? McQuail, D in Siune, K.(ed.): *Media Policy. Convergence, Concentration and Commerce*. London: Sage Publications.

Keene, Karlyn (1990): *Monitoring Media Attitudes.* American Enterprise, July-August.

Kelly, Mary in Truetzschler, Wolfgang (1997): 'Ireland', 110–125. V: Bernt Stubbe Ostergard (ed.): *The media in Western Europe. The Euromedia Handbook.* London: Sage.

Kleinsteuber, Hans J. (1997): 'Federal Republic of Germany (FRG)', 7–97. V: Bernt Stubbe Ostergard (ur.): *The media in Western Europe. The Euromedia Handbook.* London: Sage.

Klopfenstein, Bruce, C., in Sedman, David (1990): Technical standards and the marketplace: The case of AM stereo. V: *Journal of Broadcasting and Electronic Media,* 34(2), 171–194.

Kumar, Krisham (1989): Public Service Broadcsting and the Public Interest. V: *The BBC and Public Service Broadcasting* (ed. C. MacCabe in O. Stewart). Manchester: University of Manchester Press.

Kung-Shankleman, Lucy (2000): *Inside the BBC and CNN. Managing Media Organisations.* London: Routledge.

Lacy, Stephen, Sohn; Ardyth, B., in Wicks, Jan, L. (1993): *Media management: A casebook approach.* Mahwah: Lawrence Erlbaum Associate.

Lambert, Stephen (1982): *Channel Four.* London: BFI Publishing.

Lambeth, Edmund (1986): *Ethics in Media Communication.* Oxford: Oxford University Press.

Lavine, John, D., in Wackman, Daniel, B. (1988): *Managing media organizations: Effective leadership of the media.* New York: Longman.

Lazarsfeld, Paul F. in Merton, Robert (1948): 'Mass communication, popular taste and organized social action', 95–118. V: Lyman Bryson (ur.): *The communication of ideas.* New York: Harper.

McKinsey & Company (1999): *Public Service Broadcasters around the world: A McKinsey Report for the BBC.* London: McKinsey & Company.

McKinsey & Company (2013): Global media report. McKinsey & Company.

McLuhan, Marshall, (1964): *Understanding Media.* London: Routledge and Kegan Page.

McLuhan, Marshall in Powers, Bruce R. (1998): *The Global Village: Transformation in World Life and Media in the 21st Century.* New York: Oxford University Press.

McManus, Judith (1994): *Market-driven journalism:Let the citizen beware?* Newbury Park: Sage.

McManus, Judith (1992): Serving the public and serving the market: A conflict of interest? V:*Journal of Mass Media Ethics,* 7(4), 196–208.

McQuail, Denis (2001): "*Mass communication theory*", 4the edition. London: SAGE Publications.

McQuail, Denis in Karen Siune (eds. for the Euromedia Research Group) (1998): *Media policy. Convergence, concentration & commerce.* London: Sage.

McQuail, Denis. (1992): "*Media Performance*". London: SAGE Publications.

McQuail, Dennis (1984): *Communication, Social processes.* London-New York: Longman.

McQuail, Dennis (1991): *Electronic Media Policy in Western Europe.* Amsterdam: Cramwinckel.

Mitchell, Jeremy in Blumler, Jay, G. (ur.), (1994): *Television and the Viewer Interest.* London: John Libey (European Institute for the Media).

Negrine, Ralph (1985): *Great Britain: The End of Public Service Tradition?* London-Sidney: Croom Helm.

Negrine, Ralph (1992): *Politics and the Mass Media in Britain.* London: Routledge and Kegan Paul.

Negroponte, Nicholas (1996): *Being digital.* New York: Knopf.

Nielsen Media Research (2000): *2000 report on television.* New York: Author.

Nobre-Correia, Jose-Manuel (1997): 'Portugal', str. 185–193. V: Bernt Stubbe Řstergard (ed.): *The media in Western Europe.* The Euromedia Handbook. London: Sage.

Oster, Sharon, M. (1994): *Management of non-profit organizations.* Aldershot: Datmouth Publishing.

Ouchi, William G. (1981): *Theory Z: How American business can meet the Japanese challenge.* Reading: Addison-Wesley.

Owen, Bruce M. (1979): *Television economics.* Lexington: Heath.

Petersen, Vibeke G. and Siune, Karen (1997): 'Denmark', str. 35–47. V: Bernt Stubbe Řstergard (ur.): *The media in Western Europe. The Euromedia Handbook.* London: Sage.

Piccard, Robert (1989): *Media economics: Concepts and issues.* Beverly Hills: Sage.

Piccard, Robert (2002): "Assesing Audience Performance of PSB". V: *European Journal of Communication,* No. 2, str. 22.

Piccard, Robert (1998): *"Evolving Media Markets: Effects of Economic and Policy Changes"*. Turku: Turku School of Economics.

Porter, Vincent (1995): The New European Order for Public Service Broadcasting. V: Eric Barendt et al. (ed.): *The Yearbook of Media and Entertainment Law 1995*. Oxford and New York: Clarendon Press, p.p. 81–00.

Porter, Vincent (2002): Public Service Broadcasting in Europe; lecture at *European Summer School in Communication*, avgust. London: University of Westminster.

Porter, Vincent (2003): predavanje na AHRB, Centre for British Film and Television Studies, doktorski in postdoktorski seminar; Komunikacijska politika, 13–14. marec. London: Keynes Library.

Pringle, Peter, Starr, Michael, & McCavitt, William (1999): *Electronic media management* (4th ed.). Boston: Focal Press.

Quaal, Ward L. (1976): *Broadcast management*. New York: Hastings House.

Raboy, Marc (1997): Public Service Broadcasting in the Context of Globalisation (p. 77–88). In: Atkinson, Dave and Raboy, Marc: *Public Servis Broadcsting: the Challenges of the Twenty first Century*. UNESCO: Reports and Papers.

Reith, John C. W. (1924): *Broadcast over Britain*. London: Hodder and Stroughton.

Rothbard, Murray N. (1994): *For a New Liberty: The Libertarian Manifesto*. San Francisco: Fox & Wilkes.

Rubin, Bernard (1978): *Questioning Media Ethics*. New York: Praeger Publishers.

Siune, Karen in Hulten, Olof (1998): "Does public broadcasting have a future?" In: McQuail, Denis in Siune, Karen (ed.): *Media Policy*. London: Sage, p. 22–38.

Splichal, Slavko (1992): *Izgubljene utopije*. Ljubljana: Znanstveno in publicističo središče.

Survey Profiles Voters' use of Media, Media Studies Center, Freedom Forum News Advisory, na: http://www.medias.studies.org/new.html

Tapper, Helena (1997): 'Finland', 48–55. V: Bernt Stubbe Řstergard (ed.): *The media in Western Europe. The Euromedia Handbook*. London: Sage.

Taylor, W. Frederick (1991): *The Principles of Scientific Management*. New York: Harper & Row.

The Billett Consultancy (1999): *The Implications for Commercial Television from Advertising*. London.

Funding of BBC. The Billett Consultancy za ITV. London.

The Broadcasting Act (1990). HMSO.

Congresional Budget Office *(1999): The Economics and Budget Outlook: An Update*, July 1.

The failure of new media (2000, August 19). V: *The Economist*, str. 53–55.

The Public Service Idea. The Broadcasting Research Unit (1985). BRU.

Thelen, David (1996): *Becoming Citizens in the Age of Televison*. Chicago: University of Chicago Press.

Tjernstrom, Sune (2002): Theorethical Approaches to the management of the Public Service Media Firm. V: *Journal of Media Economics*, 15 (4), str. 241–258.

Tracey, Michael (1998): *The Decline and Fall of Public Service Broadcasting*. Oxford: Oxford University Press.

Tunstall, Jeremy (1971*): "Journalists at Work"*. London: Constable.

Tunstall, Jeremy (1991): "A media Industry Perspective". In: James A. Anderson (ed.): *Communication Yearbook* 14. Newbury Park: Sage. p. 163–186.

TV viewing in Internet households. (1999) Nielsen Media Research. Na spletnih straneh: http://www.nielsenmedia.com.

Union europeennen de radio-television (1993): *Les services publics de radiodiffusion en Europe:Tendances*. Pourquoi l'avdiovisuel public. Analyse economique. Bruxelles.

Van Cuilenburg, Jan and McQuail, Denis (1998): Media Policy Paradigm Shifts: V: *Search of a New Communications Policy Paradigm*. Edited by Picard, R. G. *Evolving media markets: Effects of Economic and policy Changes*. Turku: The Economic research Foundation for Mass Communication.

Van Cuilenburg, Jan and Slaa, Paul (1993): "From Media Policy toward a National Communications Policy: Broadening the Scope". V: *European Journal of Communication*, 8, str. 149–176.

Veljanovski, Cento (1996): *Privatisation of Channel 4*. London: European Media Forum.

Veronis, Suhler, & Associates (1999): *Communications industry forecast, 1999–2003*. New York: Author.

Wieten, Jan, Murdock, Graham and Dahlgren, Peter (2000): "*Television Across Europe*." London: Sage Publications.

Woldt, Runar and Dries, Josephine, Gerber, Arnaud in Konert, Bertram (1998): *Perspectives of Public Service Television in Europe.* Dusseldorf: The European Institute for the Media.

World Almanac and Book of Facts 2002 (2002): *World Almanac Books.* New York.

World Almanac and Book of Facts 2014 (2014): *World Almanac Books.* New York.

Zenith Media (2001): *UK Television Forecasts to 2006.* Zenith Media. London.

Zolnierek, James; Rangos, Katie in Eisner, James (1999, March): *Long distance market shares, fourth quarter 1998.* Washington, DC: Industry Analysis Division, Common Carrier Bureau, Federal Communications Commission. Web pages: http://www.fcc.gov/ccb/stats

Žilič Fišer, Suzana (2007): Upravljanje televizije. Fakulteta za družbene vede, Univerza v Ljubljani

Žilič Fišer, Suzana. The management of a hybrid broadcasting model: reconciling public and commercial interests. V: BADILLO, Patrick-Yves (ur.), LESOURD, Jean-Baptiste (ur.). *The media industries and their markets: quantitative analyses,* (Applied Econometrics Association series). Basingstoke: Palgrave Macmillan, 2010, str. 49–63.

Žurga, Gordana (1997): *Načela novega upravljanja javnega sektorja in državna uprava.* V: *Zbornik 16. Posvetovanje organizatorjev dela: Quo vadis management.* Kranj: Moderna organizacija. p. 470–476.

Žurga, Gordana (2000): *Zagotavljanje in spremljanje uspešnosti in učinkovitosti v državni upravi.* Ljubljana: FDV. PhD thesis.

http://cyberatlas.internet.com/big_picture/geographics/article/0,1323,5911_594751,00.html

http://www.cpb.org/annualreports/

http://europa.eu.int/

http://hillsource.house.gov

www.bbc.co.uk

www.channel4.co.uk

www.culture.gov.uk

www.fcc.gov

www.fcc.gov/mmb/cco

www.fullerton.edu/les/ethics_list.html

www.journalism.sfsu.edu/www/ethics.html

www.nab.com

www.newsling.org/

www.nielsenmedia.com

www.pbs.org/mediamatters

www.people-press.org/tech96sum.htm

www.sriresearch.com

www.truthinmedia.org

www.uta.fi/ethicnet

www.ebu.ch

www.efqm.org/model_awards/model

Tables and Figures

Table 1: Diversity of UK programmes

*Table : Diversity of television genres in "primetime"-u (18:00 – 22:30)**

	Network BBC TV	**BBC 1**	**BBC 2**	**ITV/C4/ C5**	**ITV**	**C4**	**C5**
Films	*						
Drama	*	*		*	*		*
Original english series	*	*		*	*		
Long-run series	*	*		*	*	*	*
Original english series	*	*	*				
Other comedies	*		*	*		*	
Enternteinmemt shows				*		*	
Quiz shows	*	*	*	*	*	*	
Family shows	*	*		*	*		*
Sport	*	*	*	*	*	*	*
Informative programme	*	*		*	*	*	*
Regional news	*	*		*	*		
Current affairs news	*		*	*			
Customer shows	*	*					
Arts programme	*		*				
Leisure shows	*	*	*	*	*	*	
Natural sciences shows	*	*	*	*			*
Scientific and medical programme	*	*	*	*		*	
Shows about people	*	*	*	*	*	*	*
Popular music	*	*	*	*		*	*
Classical music	*		*	*			
Religion programme	*						
Together 2001/2002	**21**	**15**	**12**	**17**	**10**	**10**	**8**

Source: BARB (2000)

Table 2: Shares of different genres at peak hours

	Drama programme	Enterntain-ment programme	Current affairs and education programme	Information programme and weather	Sport	Regionalne programme	Arts pro-gramme	Religion programme
1997 BBC1	25	26	21	18	2	6,5	0	1,5
2001 BBC1	24,5	24,5	22	17	3	8	0,5	0,5
1997 ITV	50,5	19,5	7	8	3	12	0	0
2001 ITV	42	26	6	12	3,5	10,5	0	0
1997 BBC2	23	17	39,5	1,5	13	1	5	0
2001 BBC2	20,5	24	41	0,5	10	0,5	3	0,5
1997 Channel 4	31	22	30	14	1	0	2	0
2001 Channel 4	25	23,7	29	17	4	0	0,5	0,8
1997 Channel 5	50,5	11	22	11	5,5	0	0	0
2001 Channel 5	53	11	17	12,5	6	0	0,5	0

Source: ITC Annual Reports (1997–2001)

Table 3: Special requirements from ITC

	Required 2001	**Reached 2001**	**Reached 2000**	**Reached 1999**	**Reached 1998**	**Reached 1997**
Own production	60%	69%	66%	60%	57%	N/A
Independent production	25%	61%	66%	76%	88%	83%
European production	50+%	73%	70%	65%	62%	63%
Repeats (max)	40%	39%	38%	38%	43%	42%
Subtitling	111 h/ week	136 h/ week	116 h/ week	101 h/ week	–	–
Production outside London	30%	29%	29%	27%	26%	25%

Source: Reports ITC and Channel 4 (1997–2000)

Table 4: Average daily viewing share by population groups

		Individuals	**Adults ABC1**	**Adults C2DE**	**Adults 16–34**	**Adults 55+**	**Adults 35–54**	**Children**	**Men**	**Women**
1997	1730-2359	8,95	9,49	8,6	10,95	7,84	8,94	8,73	8,8	9,08
	0600-2359	10,6	10,82	10,69	11,5	10,84	10,01	9,59	10,59	10,62
1998	1730-2359	8,8	9,58	8,32	10,94	7,86	8,53	8,27	8,51	9,05
	0600-2359	10,33	10,9	10,32	11,45	10,71	9,55	8,64	10,12	10,51
1999	1730-2359	8,92	9,83	8,4	11,16	7,86	8,64	8,82	8,9	8,93
	0600-2359	10,26	11,1	10,22	11,59	10,7	9,54	8,23	10,44	10,11
2000	1730-2359	9,34	10,57	8,54	12,52	7,56	9,1	8,82	9,25	9,41
	0600-2359	10,49	11,57	10,26	12,59	10,36	9,81	8,23	10,75	10,26
2001	1730-2359	9,16	10,63	8,32	12,6	7,22	9,21	7,76	9,2	9,14
	0600-2359	9,98	11,28	9,72	11,96	9,97	9,5	7,01	10,34	9,66

Source: Reports from Channel 4 (1997–2001)

Table 5: Viewing of different genres by population groups

	Daily	Weekly	Monthly
Housewifes	40,5%	77,8%	88,7%
Adults	37,5%	75,0%	87,5%
Adults ABC1	36,2%	75,0%	87,6%
Adults 16–24	31,1%	66,5%	82,5%
Men	36,9%	74,2%	86,7%
Children	22,1%	61,4%	83,5%
Housewifes with children	34,5%	74,4%	87,6%

Source: BARB (2001)

Table 6: Employees of Channel 4

	1997	1998	1999	2000	2001
Channel 4	520	535	686	687	724
4 Ventures	100	139	122	247	357
Together	*620*	*674*	*808*	*934*	*1.081*
men	260	289	358	408	488
women	360	385	450	526	593
Together	*620*	*674*	*808*	*934*	*1.081*
full time employment	566	626	746	901	1.034
part time	54	48	62	33	47
Together	*620*	*674*	*808*	*934*	*1.081*
Sales department	97	106	97	111	116

Source: Reports from Channel 4 (1997–2001)

Table 7: Income, employees

	1997	1998	1999	2000	2001
mio GBP	513,4	559,6	600,5	651,7	619,4
employment	620	674	808	934	1.081

Source: Channel 4 Annual reports (1997–2001)

Table 8: Employees and programme quantities

	1997	1998	1999	2000	2001
hours	8.734	8.760	8.760	8.784	8.760
mio GBP	310,2	351	390,6	425,6	425,5
emply	620	674	808	934	1.081

Source: Channel 4 Annual reports (1997–2001)

Table 9: Advertising

v mio GBP	1993	1994	1995	1996	1997	1998	1999	2000	2001
Channel 4	330,10	393,90	448,00	490,40	513,40	559,60	600,50	651,70	619,40
ITV, GMTV, S4C, Channel 5	1.483,10	1.602,70	1.693,40	1.762,20	1.876,80	2.023,00	2.176,90	2.315,70	2.012,40
	1.813,20	1.996,60	2.141,40	2.252,60	2.390,20	2.582,60	2.777,40	2.967,40	2.631,80

Source: ITC Annual reports (1993–2001)

Figure 2: Organizational structure of Channel 4 for 2001

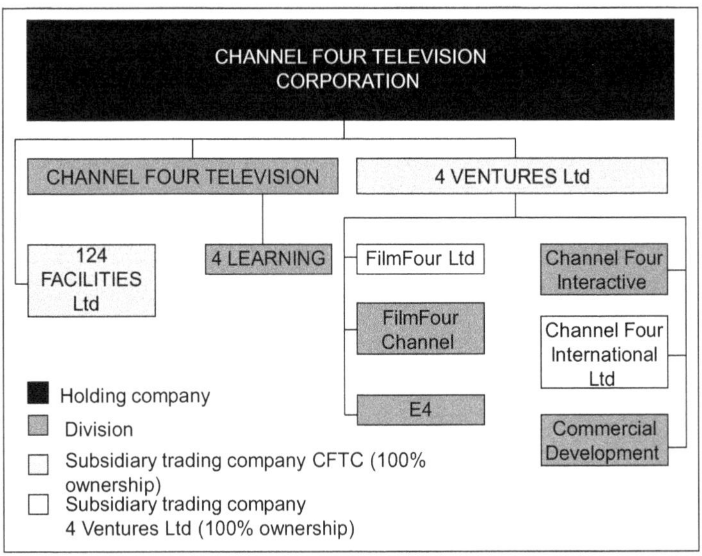

Source: Channel 4

Figure 3: Sources of income for RTV Slovenija, 2010 (RTV Annual report, 2011)

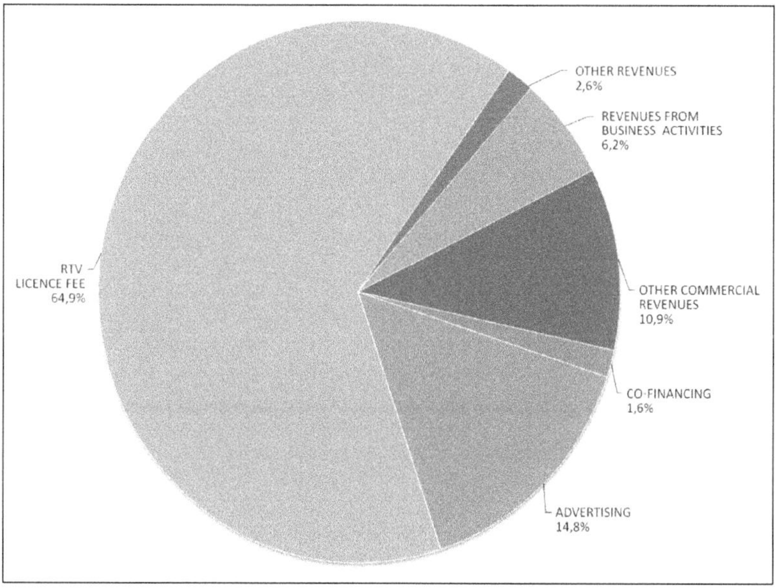

Figure 4: Sources of income for RTV Slovenija, 2013 (RTV Annual report, 2013)

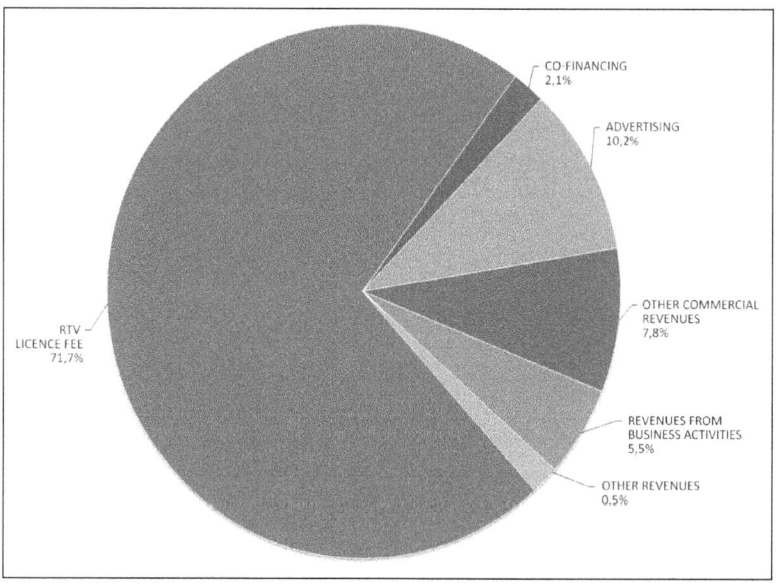

www.ingramcontent.com/pod-product-compliance
Ingram Content Group UK Ltd.
Pitfield, Milton Keynes, MK11 3LW, UK
UKHW021011120926
8556IPUK00039B/994

9 783631 663066